Praise for *Decide & Conquer*:

"Do you have trouble making important decisions? If you answered, 'Well, yes and no,' you need this book. It's as smart and straightforward as its title. I'm buying my agent five copies.

—Joel Siegel
Entertainment Editor
Good Morning America

"I thought making decisions was as natural as breathing— something we just do. Dr. Robbins makes it crystal clear that decision making ability is a skill that can be improved with knowledge from self evaluation and consideration of the right criteria. This book will help not only people who struggle with decisions, but also those who consider themselves effective decision makers."

—Jim Despain, Managing Partner,
DESPAINCONVERSE, and co-author
of *...and Dignity for All*

"Robbins shows that making good decisions requires more than just knowing the facts. You must know yourself, too! It is the human aspects of the decision-making process that fail. But these problems can be overcome. Start making good decisions now by choosing to read this book."

—John Nofsinger, author of
Infectious Greed and Investment Blunders
(of the Rich and Famous)

"A must read. Robbins translates a vast array of arcane research into a clearly written practical guide that will surely help people make better personal decisions."

—Steven P. Schnaars, author of
Marketing Strategy, Second Edition

"This is a very personal book that has shown me how to make better choices in my life. The chapter on "Over Confidence" explains why I made some not so good choices and has changed the way I will make decisions from here on out."

—Michael Basch, co-founder, FedEx,
and author of *Customerculture: How FedEx
and Other Great Companies Put the Customer
First Every Day*

"I loved this book. It is fun, easy to read and has ideas that can be instantly applied. *Decide & Conquer* should be required reading for the leaders of the future! It provides a roadmap that can help leaders make better decisions. It is also a coaching tool that leaders can use to help others make better decisions."

> —Marshall Goldsmith, co-editor of
> *Coaching for Leadership. Listed in Forbes*
> *as one of five top executive coaches and in*
> *The Wall Street Journal as a "top ten"*
> executive educator

"Don't wait until you have a big decision to make to read this book. *Decide & Conquer* is full of provocative information to help you to understand yourself better, rationally break down any size problem and move on with your life goals. This book is thoughtful and enlightening and as Dr. Robbins reminds us, ignorance isn't bliss."

> —Joanne Cini, Former SVP
> Sales & Marketing,
> NBC TV Stations

"This book is a page-turner! It will teach you more about making better decisions than almost anything you'll ever read. A must read for anyone who wants to improve their decision making process."

> —Jason Jennings, worldwide bestselling
> author of *Less Is More* and
> *It's Not The Big That Eat*
> *The Small—It's The Fast*
> *That Eat The Slow*

"Good Decisions can form a solid foundation for a good life and career. If you want to know the state of the art on making good decisions then make the very good decision to read *Decide & Conquer* at your earliest opportunity."

> —Charles C. Manz, bestselling author of
> *Emotional Discipline and*
> *The New SuperLeadership*

"Conversational yet penetrating, qualitative yet analytical, Stephen Robbins paints a portrait of decision making processes. While the focus of this book strives to super charge decision making skills for individuals, perhaps its greatest use is in allowing leaders to best interpret the recommendations of individuals and teams."

> —Kevin Kennedy, COO,
> Openwave Systems Inc.
> and author of *Going the Distance:*
> *Why Some Companies*
> *Dominate and Others Fail*

"This book makes a vast body of very important and useful research on human decision processes available to business readers in very accessible style; it should reach a wide audience and have real impact on how decisions get made."

—Rob Austin, Harvard Business School,
and co-author of *Artful Making:*
What Managers Can Learn
from How Artists Work

"For business leaders, knowing what to focus on and what to let go, is essential. Robbins delivers an fun read with a great set of tools and tips for doing so."

—Amir Hartman, CEO,
Mainstay Partners, and
author of *Ruthless Execution:*
What Business Leaders Do When
Their Company Hits the Wall

"Decisions! Decisions! Decisions! We make hundreds of them everyday. Finally, a book has been written that provides us with simple, yet concrete knowledge to help us make better choices in our lives. If you want to make better decisions to improve all aspects of your life, then buy this book."

—Christopher Neck
Associate Professor,
Department of Management,
Virginia Tech

"Brilliant insights. I wish, when I was deciding to start my own company, that I had known about Robbins. It would have saved me a lot of sleepless nights. Powerful advice on decision making."

—Erica Orloff, novelist and author of
The 60-Second Commute:
A Guide to Your 24/7 Home Office Life

"Upbeat, positive and empowering; *Decide & Conquer* is *the* road map to better decision making in both your personal and business life."

—Cleo Coy, Former Director of Buying,
Waldenbooks

"Turning the pages of his latest book, it is easy to see why Stephen Robbins is the world's leading authority on business management. He gets wiser with every book he writes."

—Kathy Levinson, Ph.D.
The 60-Second Commute

Decide &
Conquer

Decide & Conquer

Make Winning Decisions and Take Control of Your Life

Stephen P. Robbins, Ph.D.

Prentice Hall
FINANCIAL TIMES

An Imprint of PEARSON EDUCATION
Upper Saddle River, NJ • New York • London • San Francisco • Toronto • Sydney
Tokyo • Singapore • Hong Kong • Cape Town • Madrid
Paris • Milan • Munich • Amsterdam

www.ft-ph.com

Library of Congress Cataloging-in-Publication Data

Robbins, Stephen P.
    Decide & conquer: make winning decisions and take control of your life /
Stephen P. Robbins.
    p cm.
    Includes bibliographical references and index.
    ISBN 0-13-142501-3
       1. Decision making. I. Title: Decide and conquer. II. Title.

BF448.R63 2003
658.4'03--dc21

2003048728

Editorial/production supervision: *Nicholas Radhuber*
Executive editor: *Tim Moore*
Editorial assistant: *Richard Winkler*
Marketing manager: *Alexis R. Heydt-Long*
Manufacturing buyer: *Maura Zaldivar*
Cover design director: *Jerry Votta*
Cover design: *Anthony Gemmellaro*
Art director: *Gail Cocker-Bogusz*
Interior design: *Meg Van Arsdale*

© 2004 Pearson Education, Inc.
Publishing as Financial Times Prentice Hall
Upper Saddle River, New Jersey 07458

Financial Times Prentice Hall books are widely used by corporations and
government agencies for training, marketing, and resale.

**Prentice Hall offers excellent discounts on this book when ordered in quantity for bulk
purchases or special sales. For more information, please contact:
U.S. Corporate and Government Sales
1-800-382-3419
corpsales@pearsontechgroup.com**

**For sales outside of the U.S., please contact:
International Sales
1-317-581-3793
international@pearsontechgroup.com**

Company and product names mentioned herein are the trademarks
or registered trademarks of their respective owners.

Printed in the United States of America

1st Printing.

ISBN 0-13-142501-3

Pearson Education LTD.
Pearson Education Australia PTY, Limited
Pearson Education Singapore, Pte. Ltd.
Pearson Education North Asia Ltd.
Pearson Education Canada, Ltd.
Pearson Educación de Mexico, S.A. de C.V.
Pearson Education—Japan
Pearson Education Malaysia, Pte. Ltd.

FINANCIAL TIMES PRENTICE HALL BOOKS

For more information, please go to www.ft-ph.com

Business and Technology
Sarv Devaraj and Rajiv Kohli
The IT Payoff: Measuring the Business Value of Information Technology Investments
Nicholas D. Evans
Business Agility: Strategies for Gaining Competitive Advantage through Mobile Business Solutions
Nicholas D. Evans
Business Innovation and Disruptive Technology: Harnessing the Power of Breakthrough Technology…for Competitive Advantage
Nicholas D. Evans
Consumer Gadgets: 50 Ways to Have Fun and Simplify Your Life with Today's Technology…and Tomorrow's
Faisal Hoque
The Alignment Effect: How to Get Real Business Value Out of Technology
Thomas Kern, Mary Cecelia Lacity, and Leslie P. Willcocks
Netsourcing: Renting Business Applications and Services Over a Network

Ecommerce
Dale Neef
E-procurement: From Strategy to Implementation

Economics
David Dranove
What's Your Life Worth? Health Care Rationing…Who Lives? Who Dies? Who Decides?
John C. Edmunds
Brave New Wealthy World: Winning the Struggle for World Prosperity
David R. Henderson
The Joy of Freedom: An Economist's Odyssey
Jonathan Wight
Saving Adam Smith: A Tale of Wealth, Transformation, and Virtue

Entrepreneurship
Oren Fuerst and Uri Geiger
From Concept to Wall Street: A Complete Guide to Entrepreneurship and Venture Capital
David Gladstone and Laura Gladstone
Venture Capital Handbook: An Entrepreneur's Guide to Raising Venture Capital, Revised and Updated
Erica Orloff and Kathy Levinson, Ph.D.
The 60-Second Commute: A Guide to Your 24/7 Home Office Life
Jeff Saperstein and Daniel Rouach
Creating Regional Wealth in the Innovation Economy: Models, Perspectives, and Best Practices

Finance

Aswath Damodaran
> *The Dark Side of Valuation: Valuing Old Tech, New Tech, and New Economy Companies*

Kenneth R. Ferris and Barbara S. Pécherot Petitt
> *Valuation: Avoiding the Winner's Curse*

International Business

Peter Marber
> *Money Changes Everything: How Global Prosperity Is Reshaping Our Needs, Values, and Lifestyles*

Fernando Robles, Françoise Simon, and Jerry Haar
> *Winning Strategies for the New Latin Markets*

Investments

Zvi Bodie and Michael J. Clowes
> *Worry-Free Investing: A Safe Approach to Achieving Your Lifetime Goals*

Harry Domash
> *Fire Your Stock Analyst! Analyzing Stocks on Your Own*

Philip Jenks and Stephen Eckett, Editors
> *The Global-Investor Book of Investing Rules: Invaluable Advice from 150 Master Investors*

Charles P. Jones
> *Mutual Funds: Your Money, Your Choice. Take Control Now and Build Wealth Wisely*

D. Quinn Mills
> *Buy, Lie, and Sell High: How Investors Lost Out on Enron and the Internet Bubble*

D. Quinn Mills
> *Wheel, Deal, and Steal: Deceptive Accounting, Deceitful CEOs, and Ineffective Reforms*

John Nofsinger and Kenneth Kim
> *Infectious Greed: Restoring Confidence in America's Companies*

John R. Nofsinger
> *Investment Blunders (of the Rich and Famous)…And What You Can Learn from Them*

John R. Nofsinger
> *Investment Madness: How Psychology Affects Your Investing…And What to Do About It*

Leadership

Jim Despain and Jane Bodman Converse
> *And Dignity for All: Unlocking Greatness through Values-Based Leadership*

Marshall Goldsmith, Vijay Govindarajan, Beverly Kaye, and Albert A. Vicere
> *The Many Facets of Leadership*

Marshall Goldsmith, Cathy Greenberg, Alastair Robertson, and Maya Hu-Chan
> *Global Leadership: The Next Generation*

Stephen P. Robbins
Decide & Conquer: Make Winning Decisions and Take Control of Your Life

Stephen P. Robbins
The Truth About Managing People…And Nothing but the Truth

Ronald Snee and Roger Hoerl
Leading Six Sigma: A Step-by-Step Guide Based on Experience with GE and Other Six Sigma Companies

Susan E. Squires, Cynthia J. Smith, Lorna McDougall, and William R. Yeack
Inside Arthur Andersen: Shifting Values, Unexpected Consequences

Jerry Weissman
Presenting to Win: The Art of Telling Your Story

Marketing

Michael Basch
CustomerCulture: How FedEx and Other Great Companies Put the Customer First Every Day

Deirdre Breakenridge
Cyberbranding: Brand Building in the Digital Economy

Jonathan Cagan and Craig M. Vogel
Creating Breakthrough Products: Innovation from Product Planning to Program Approval

James W. Cortada
21st Century Business: Managing and Working in the New Digital Economy

Al Lieberman, with Patricia Esgate
The Entertainment Marketing Revolution: Bringing the Moguls, the Media, and the Magic to the World

Tom Osenton
Customer Share Marketing: How the World's Great Marketers Unlock Profits from Customer Loyalty

Bernd H. Schmitt, David L. Rogers, and Karen Vrotsos
There's No Business That's Not Show Business: Marketing in Today's Experience Culture

Yoram J. Wind and Vijay Mahajan, with Robert Gunther
Convergence Marketing: Strategies for Reaching the New Hybrid Consumer

Public Relations

Gerald R. Baron
Now Is Too Late: Survival in an Era of Instant News

Deirdre Breakenridge and Thomas J. DeLoughry
The New PR Toolkit: Strategies for Successful Media Relations

Strategy

Thomas L. Barton, William G. Shenkir, and Paul L. Walker
Making Enterprise Risk Management Pay Off: How Leading Companies Implement Risk Management

Henry A. Davis and William W. Sihler
Financial Turnarounds: Preserving Enterprise Value

For Frenchy:

Every day I'm reminded that asking you to marry me remains one of the best decisions I ever made.

Contents

Preface

Few issues so widely affect our daily lives as dramatically as does the quality of our decisions. How much you earn, your health status, your relationships, and your overall level of happiness are just a sampling of outcomes that are largely due to decisions you've made.

In spite of the importance of making good decisions, few of us have had any formal training in the process. You couldn't graduate from high school without classes in English, math, science, government, and history, but did you have any courses in decision making? Probably not. If you want to be good at cooking, you take courses in cooking. The same is true for drawing, doing financial analysis, or healing the sick. Most of us even took a formal class in typing to develop our proficiency for such a mundane task as key-boarding. But, for some reason, it's just assumed that, through practice and experience, all of us can learn to be good decision makers.

A little observation tells us rather quickly that everyone doesn't make good decisions. Apparently, practice and experience aren't very good teachers of this skill. I, for one, continue to be amazed at the bad decisions some people make. They buy stocks at their peak prices and sell them when they're near their lows. They play slot machines and bet on other games of chance as if there is such a thing as a "hot streak," or they marry a person that they know is wrong for them. (For evidence on this last point, watch some of the daytime talk shows and listen to guests contrive explanations for staying with partners who continually lie and cheat on them.)

We know a great deal about how people make decisions and how to improve the process. Unfortunately, this knowledge is not widespread. The purpose of *Decide & Conquer* is to change that. Drawing on thousands of research studies, this book translates what experts know about behavioral decision processes into layman terms with heavy emphasis on application. I wrote this book as an everyman's guide on how to improve the choices that shape our lives, and, after reading this book, you will have the tools to make better decisions.

What qualifies me to write this book? I've been researching and writing about organizational decision making for nearly 30 years. My textbook on organizational behavior, for instance, is now in its 10th edition and has been read by more than a million students. The behavioral decision-making literature is a fundamental component in understanding organizational behavior. I wrote *Decide & Conquer* because I thought I could bring my "translating" skills to the behavioral decision-making literature and make this literature more accessible to people with a nontechnical background.

Keep in mind that giving you the tools to make *better* decisions is not the same as helping you to make the *right* decisions. This book is designed to show you the right way to structure and analyze problems. It focuses on the process you use to arrive at your decisions. That's because a good decision should be judged by the process used, not the results achieved. In some cases, a "good decision" results in an undesirable outcome. If you used the right process, however, you will have made a good decision regardless of the outcome. So I can't tell you *what* to decide, but I can show you *how* to decide. Unfortunately, because chance events influence outcomes, there can be no assurances that using the right process will result in a desirable outcome, but it does increase that probability.

This book has been organized into five parts. Part I argues that decision making permeates everything we do and that all of us need to know the right way to make decisions. Part II proposes that improving your decision making begins by understanding your personality traits and how they shape your decision-making preferences. Part III describes, in detail, biases and shortcuts that many of us use that hinder our decision-making effectiveness. Part IV describes a number of insights that can help you improve your decision making. Part V is a one-chapter brief summary of what you should have gotten out of reading this book.

A book like this owes its existence to two distinct sets of contributors. First are those scholars who have studied the psychology of human judgment and decision making and have shared their research with us. The insights you'll find in this book are the culmination of decades of research by hundreds of scholars such as Daniel Kahneman, Amos Tversky, Herbert A. Simon, Baruch Fischhoff, and Paul Slovic. My role here is similar to that played by television news anchors. TV news anchors don't make the news; they just report it. Similarly, I didn't "make" the findings you'll read about in this book; I merely report them. My contribution was to review the thousands of studies that have been done on behavioral decision making and translate them into a form that can be easily understood and used.

The second set of contributors are the people at my publisher-- FinancialTimes/Prentice Hall. Tim Moore, John Pierce, and Gary June believed in this project from its beginning and have provided me with terrific editorial and marketing support. Russ Hall provided feedback on how the manuscript could be improved, and Nicholas Radhuber was instrumental in managing the production process that turned my manuscript into the book you have in your hands. My thanks to each of you for making this book a reality.

Stephen P. Robbins
Seattle, Washington

Part One

Introduction

Decision Making Shapes
Your Life

You know how it is. You're 21 or 22,
and you make some decisions;
then—whish! —you're 70.
—T. Wilder

Your typical day is full of decisions. What time should I get up in the morning? Should I wear black shoes or brown shoes? What will I have for breakfast? Do I fill up the car with gas this morning or do it on the way home from work? When I get to work, what do I do first: respond to email, go through my in basket, listen to my voicemail, meet with colleagues?

Throughout your workday, you're confronted with dozens more of these mundane decisions. And *after* work, you get no rest from making choices. Do I make dinner at home or eat out? What am I in the mood for? When will I read the newspaper and go through my personal mail? Do I want to watch TV tonight, and, if so, what shows do I watch? Should I make a few calls to family and friends?

Every once in a while, your unrelenting life of routine decisions is interrupted by the need to make a major decision. For instance, your car's transmission goes out, and you have to decide whether to spend $1,500 to repair it or to go looking for a new car. The person you've been dating wants you to give up your apartment and move in together. Your employer is making cutbacks, your boss advises you that your position is being eliminated, and suddenly you've got to find a new job.

There are few activities more encompassing and characteristic of mankind than making decisions. None of us have the option to live a life void of making choices. In fact, one of the primary tasks parents have in raising children is preparing them to make decisions on their own.

> *Who you are and what you'll become (or have become) are largely determined by your decision choices.*

Decision making covers a wide territory. It encompasses everything from major decisions, such as accepting a marriage proposal, to the routine choices of everyday life like selecting among food items at the grocery store. Interestingly, most people think of decision making in the context of the *big* choices—marriage, children, college, jobs, home purchases. Yet the dozens of *day-to-day* decisions we all make can be powerful forces in shaping our lives. The person who has trouble scheduling his or her time often ends up being chronically late to work, to meetings, and to social events. It begins to interfere with job performance ratings and personal relationships. What appears on the surface to be minor decisions—what time do I get up in the morning or leave for a date—leads to losing a job or alienating a friend. In many cases, a person "down on his luck" is really just a person who has made some bad choices. He dropped out of school; tried drugs, believing he couldn't become addicted; made some foolish investments; failed to develop marketable job skills or to keep those skills current; procrastinated too long and missed out on a great business opportunity; failed to show up at work on time; chose to save money by not buying health insurance; didn't think it necessary to read the "small print" in the contract; or thought there was nothing wrong with drinking and driving. The choices we make—the small ones as well as the large ones—shouldn't be taken lightly. To do so places our future in the hands of fate.

A lot of us overlook the obvious fact that the choices we make shape our lives. Who you are and what you'll become (or have become) are largely determined by your decision choices. It's not luck that Oprah Winfrey, Rudy Giuliani, Bill Gates, and Tiger Woods excel in their professions. And it's not chance that smokers significantly increase the likelihood that they'll die of lung cancer or that people who save money on a regular basis are less likely to be destitute in their old age than people who don't. A lot of well-educated people, with talent and connections, have screwed up their lives because they've made bad choices. And a lot of people with very average talent and minimal opportunities have lived full and rich lives because they have learned how to make smart decisions. In actuality, what we often attribute to luck is nothing more than making the right choice at the right time. A large component of luck is good decision making. The point is: For the most part, the quality of your life is a result of the quality of your decisions.

The good news is that you can improve your decision skills. Even though these skills are critical for success in life, and most of us have had little or no formal training in how to make decisions, you're not captive to learn only through experience. The basic knowledge you need to have to become more effective at decision making can be condensed and summarized into a short, easy-to-read book, and here it is! In the following pages, you'll learn the steps for making optimum decisions and the roadblocks you need to be aware of that can detour this goal.

One caveat before you begin your journey. Perfecting your decision skills doesn't guarantee that all your decisions will come out the way you had hoped. Good decision skills focus on the *means* you use to reach a decision, not on the *ends*. You can't control outcomes. You can only control the process for arriving at those outcomes. As the old adage goes, however, the race doesn't always go to the swift nor the battle to the strong, but that's the way to bet. Improving your decision skills just *increases your chances* of winning life's races and battles.

Decision Tips

- Decision making is one of life's most important skills.

- You can improve your decision skills.

- You can control only the decision process, not the outcomes.

Chapter Two

The Search for Rationality

Get your facts first, and then you can
distort them as much as you please.
—M. Twain

Sean Norris was facing a decision that many of us faced when we were about 17 or 18 years of age. A senior in high school, Sean was trying to decide where to go to college.

Picking a college is a big decision. A tough decision. It would determine where Sean would be for the next four years and would set the direction for the rest of his life. Sean wasn't about to approach a decision like this lightly.

Sean began by listing his criteria for what he wanted in a college. He preferred some place not too far from his hometown, so he could drive home for long weekends and holidays. The school would have to have a program in accounting because he was pretty sure that was what he wanted for a major. He wanted a school with a good reputation. And Sean's folks reminded him that, if the cost was more than $5,000 a year, he better get financial aid or count on having a part-time job because that was all the help they could afford to provide. After considerable deliberation, Sean added a few more preferences to his list: someplace where at least one of his buddies was going; a favorable ratio of women to men; and an active fraternity-sorority system.

When Sean shared his list with his dad, his dad reminded him that all of these criteria weren't equally important. Cost and the availability of an accounting major, for instance, were probably a lot more important than the male:female ratio. Sean agreed, so he prioritized his criteria by weighting each on a scale from 1 to 10. Next, he used his career counselor at school, his local library, and the Internet to create a list of all the viable colleges that he might possibly consider attending. These efforts resulted in nearly 20 alternatives. Then Sean evaluated each of his 20 options. He became an "informed consumer" by reading as much as he could about each school, talking to people who had attended them, and visiting the campuses of the half-dozen or so that seemed to best fit his preferences. As he compared each college against the criteria and weights he had previously set, the strengths and weaknesses of each became evident. Finally, Sean identified the college that scored highest on his evaluation and made it his first choice.

The steps that Sean went through are referred to as the rational decision process.[1] It's called *rational* because Sean sought to make consistent, value-maximizing choices within the constraints he was given.[2]

Just as a straight line is the shortest distance between two points, rationality is the shortest distance between where you are and where you want to be.

Good decision making is built on rationality. Why? Because decisions based on logic, deliberate analysis, and the thoughtful search for complete information—rather than on gut feelings or experience--should lead to superior outcomes. The search for rationality forces you to confront and clarify your values so that your priorities will be consistent. This, in turn, provides you with the most direct path toward achievement of your life goals. Just as a straight line is the shortest distance between two points, rationality is the shortest distance between where you are and where you want to be.

Rational decision making follows six standard steps:[3]

1. *Identify and define the problem.* A problem exists when there is a discrepancy between an existing and a desired state of affairs.

2. *Identify decision criteria.* This step clarifies what is relevant or important in making the decision. This step brings the decision maker's interests, values, goals, and personal preferences into the process. More important, it's this listing of criteria that often results in two people, in similar situations, making very different choices because what one person thinks is relevant may not be relevant to the other person. In the rational process, any factor not identified in this step is considered irrelevant to the decision maker and will have no bearing on the outcome.

3. *Weight the criteria.* Because the criteria are rarely all equal in importance, the decision maker needs to weight the previously identified criteria in order to give them correct priority in the decision.

4. *Generate alternatives.* This step requires the decision maker to generate all possible alternatives that could succeed in solving the problem.

5. *Evaluate each alternative.* After the alternatives are identified, each must be critically analyzed and evaluated. This is done by rating each alternative on each criterion. The strengths and weaknesses of each alternative should become evident as they are compared with the criteria and weights established in the second and third steps.

6. *Select the choice that scores highest*. Finally, the process concludes by choosing the alternative that scores highest. This is the optimal choice.

Note that these are exactly the steps that Sean followed in making his college decision. He identified his problem: finding a college to attend. He identified and weighted the criteria he thought important in his decision. He developed a list of colleges to consider. Then he carefully evaluated each and selected the one that best met his needs.

What might Sean's decision process have looked like had he *not* sought rationality? Here are a couple of nonrational scenarios. Sean begins with an implicit favorite and then looks for reasons to reject it. He focuses singularly on one school that offers him a large financial aid package and ignores his other goals and criteria. He decides to go to a school because his best friend is going there. Or he makes his choice based only on what he read in the various colleges' catalogs. Each of these approaches increase the likelihood that Sean would regret his decision—making him unhappy and possibly transferring to another school or dropping out of college altogether.

Your goal should be to make rational decisions, especially when you're facing major, life-changing events. Throughout this book, I'll offer you suggestions to help you make your decision process more rational. However, as I show in the next chapter, there are a number of reasons why rationality is more an ideal than reality, so your quest becomes one of attempting to be as *rational as possible*.

Decision Tips

- Use the rational decision process whenever possible.
- The time and care necessary to follow the rational process is especially important when you're facing major, life-changing events.

Why It's Hard to Be Rational

*You'll never have all the information you need
to make a decision. If you did, it would be
a foregone conclusion, not a decision.*

—Anonymous

Did you cancel any air-travel plans following the September 11, 2001, terrorist attacks? Did you avoid going into skyscrapers or attending events where masses of people might be? If you did, you were probably afraid of becoming a terror victim. But was fear of terrorism immediately following 9/11 a rational response? The answer is probably no,[1] but, as you'll see in this chapter, it's hard to be rational.

A rational person would be far more fearful of dying in his or her car than becoming a terrorist-initiated air flight casualty. In fact, it's been calculated that terrorists would have to hijack 50 planes a year and kill everyone aboard before flying would be more dangerous than driving an equal distance. In spite of such statistics, people act irrationally to terrorism. Why? First, there's substantial evidence that human beings are bad at assessing small risks of large catastrophes. Second, the actual risk of being a terror victim is not merely small. It's unknowable. This makes any guess

11

potentially valid and plays into the hands of media people and politicians who might benefit from panic. And third, it's hard to be rational about the irrational. How can you understand or predict the behavior of a suicide bomber who is convinced he'll become a hero in Heaven after killing you?

In spite of very good intentions, there are barriers that make it difficult for us to be rational.[2] Those barriers start with the unrealistic assumptions that underlie rationality:[3]

- *A clear and unambiguous problem*. Rationality assumes that the decision maker fully understands the problem. In reality, problems are typically complex, with considerable ambiguity as to what's cause and what's effect. The result is that we often end up focusing on the wrong problem, confusing the problem with its symptoms, or ignoring or denying that there even is a problem.

- *All relevant criteria can be identified, as can all alternatives*. In the real world, human beings are limited in their abilities to identify criteria and alternatives. We tend to focus on the visible and obvious. In addition, our biases and personal preferences tend to restrict a full and complete listing of options.

- *Criteria and alternatives can be ranked and weighted to reflect their importance*. Because problems are typically complex, it's often hard to rank and weight criteria and alternatives objectively.

- *There are no constraints in getting full information*. Rationality assumes that we can get all the information we need to make a thorough and thoughtful choice. In reality, there are time and cost constraints that make it typically impossible to obtain full information.

- *Decision makers can accurately assess each alternative*. Rationality presumes that the decision maker has full information about each alternative and that he or she will rely only on the criteria chosen, and the weights given to those criteria, in evaluating each alternative. In the real world, full information is never available. We also find it hard to limit analysis to only the criteria identified and to rate the criteria's importance in proportion to the weights given. We often let irrelevant criteria or emotions influence our judgment.

In addition to unrealistic assumptions, there are systematic biases and errors that creep into our decision processes and undermine rationality. They come out of our attempts to short-cut the decision process. To minimize effort and to avoid difficult trade-offs, we rely too heavily on experience, impulses, gut feelings,

> *To minimize effort and avoid difficult trade-offs, we rely too heavily on experience, impulses, gut feelings, and convenient "rules of thumb."*

and convenient "rules of thumb." In many cases, these shortcuts are helpful. However, they can lead to severe distortions from rationality. I'll elaborate on many of these biases and errors later in the book, but here are some "coming attractions" of such biases and errors:

- *We don't plan ahead.* It's hard for most of us to think long-term. As a result, we tend to react to momentary impulses, act inconsistently in pursuit of our priorities, and deviate from the direct path to our goals.

- *We're overconfident.* Most of us are overconfident about our knowledge and abilities. This leads us to do too little analysis of our options and to be too optimistic about our ability to select the best choice.

- *We rely too much on past experiences.* Experience can teach us a lot, but it also tends to limit our thinking. It's especially limiting when we're faced with new or novel situations. Overreliance on experience tends to stifle the development of creative options.

- *We're poor at learning from the past*. Our memory is highly selective, and we're pretty good at reinterpreting past experiences in ways that maintain or enhance our self-esteem. Therefore, we often don't see problems when we should, and we're unrealistic in assessing past "successes" and "failures."

Rationality assumes that we can perfectly define a problem; identify all relevant criteria; accurately weigh all the criteria to reflect our goals, values, and interests; list all relevant alternatives; accurately evaluate and compare each of those alternatives; and select the best alternative. As noted before, the evidence confirms what you've always known—we're not perfect. Between the naïve assumptions underlying rationality and the imperfections of the human mind, we all act irrationally at times.

Just because we all have difficulty being rational doesn't mean we're destined to constantly screw up the decisions we have to make. In spite of our limitations, many of us actually do a pretty good job of decision making. Part of the reason is that some people have learned the tricks to "managing irrationality." By that I mean, they know their biases and have figured out how to minimize their impact. By the time you've finished reading this book, you should be a lot better at this task than you were before you began reading.

But even most people who know little about the psychology of decision making seem to get by on their limited knowledge. Why is that? First, the right or optimal choice is often obvious. Second, in many situations, a wide range of options will achieve an optimal, or nearly optimal, solution. And third, satisfactory solutions are often good enough.[4] In the real world, every decision doesn't have dozens of choices, and, when they do, most are often clearly inferior. If you're looking for a new television set, you're likely to go to a Best Buy or Wal-Mart and check out their selection. After you impose your criteria—screen size, features, cost, and so forth—a single choice will often surface. What if this process ends up creating three or four choices rather than one? In many cases, any one of those choices will prove to be just fine because the differences between them are negligible. Finally, there is substantial evidence to suggest that many decisions can be solved by merely finding a *satisficing* solution—that is, one that is satisfactory and sufficient—rather than optimizing. We search until we find the first solution that meets all our criteria, and then we select it. In contrast to Sean Norris' rational process for choosing a college, described at the opening of the last chapter, most of us satisficed. We identified criteria that we thought important in our college choice, developed a short list of possible options, and applied to the first school we found that was acceptable. For many of the decisions we face on a day-to-day basis, there is little to be gained by seeking an optimum choice. A satisfactory option proves good enough.

Unfortunately, "good enough" is often *not* good enough. When you think back about decisions that didn't work out the way you had hoped, it's often the result of having used inappropriate shortcuts and settling for a less-than-optimum choice. The remainder of this book will help you to understand both your unique preferences and biases and those commonly shared by all of us, and what you can do to improve your decision "batting average."

Decision Tips

- You can reduce many of the biases and errors that undermine rationality.

- Optimal choices are often obvious.

- In many situations, a wide range of options will achieve a near-optimal solution.

- Satisfactory solutions are often good enough.

Part Two

How Do *You* Make Decisions?

What's Your Decision Style?

Listed below are statements describing how individuals go about making important decisions. Please indicate whether you agree of disagree with each statement.[1]

	Strongly Disagree	Disagree	Neither Agree or Disagree	Agree	Strongly Agree
1. When making decisions, I rely upon my instincts.	—	—	—	—	—
2. I double-check my information sources to be sure I have the right facts before making a decision.	—	—	—	—	—
3. When I make a decision, I trust my inner feelings and reactions.	—	—	—	—	—
4. I make decisions in a logical and systematic way.	—	—	—	—	—

19

	Strongly Disagree	Disagree	Neither Agree or Disagree	Agree	Strongly Agree
5. I generally make decisions that feel right to me.	—	—	—	—	—
6. My decision making requires careful thought.	—	—	—	—	—
7. When I make a decision, it is more important for me to feel the decision is right than to have a rational reason for it.	—	—	—	—	—
8. When making a decision, I consider various options in terms of a specific goal.	—	—	—	—	—

How to Score

For the four odd-numbered questions (1,3,5,7), give yourself 1 point for each Strongly Disagree answer, 2 points for Disagree, 3 points for Neither Agree or Disagree, 4 points for Agree, and 5 points for Strongly Agree. Add up your score. Now do the same for the even-numbered questions.

Your total for the odd-numbered items represents your Intuitive score. Your total for the even-numbered items represents your Rational score.

What Your Score Means

Your scores for each style will range between 4 and 20. The style with the higher score indicates your preferred style, but also note the difference between the two scores. The greater the difference, the stronger your preferred style is in shaping how you approach decision making. If both scores are fairly close or if your scores tend to congregate around the midpoint (this would include scores of between 10 and 14), you're more flexible in how you approach decisions and may be more sensitive to seeing how differences in situations affect the choice of your decision style.

Understanding Decision-Making Style

Decision-making style refers to the habitual patterns we tend to fall back on when faced with a decision situation. Although there are a number of different ways to classify decision styles, almost all include a deliberate and logical approach (which we call rational, but which is also referred to as a thinking style) and an intuitive approach that relies on hunches and gut feelings (often called a feeling style).[2]

Your decision-making style is particularly relevant in determining how you gather information. Rational types emphasize facts, details, and rational cause-effect logic. They weigh evidence objectively and unemotionally. Well-known rationals would include Albert Einstein, Ayn Rand, and Bill Gates. Intuitive types focus on possibilities and relationships between ideas. They weigh options against their personal values more than rational logic. Well-known intuitives include Albert Schweitzer, Mikhail Gorbachev, and Eleanor Roosevelt.

Are You a Risk Taker?

For each of the following situations, indicate the minimum odds of success you would demand before recommending that one alternative be chosen over another. Try to place yourself in the position of the central person in each of the situations.[1]

1. Ben, a 45-year-old accountant, has recently been informed by his physician that he has developed a severe heart ailment. The disease is serious enough to force Ben to change many of his strongest life habits—reducing his workload, drastically changing his diet, and giving up favorite leisure-time pursuits. The physician suggests that a delicate medical operation could be attempted, which, if successful, would completely relieve the heart condition. However, its success could not be assured, and, in fact, the operation might prove fatal.

    Imagine you are advising Ben. Listed below are several probabilities or odds that the operation will prove successful. Check the *lowest probability* that you would consider acceptable for the operation to be performed.

____Place a check here if you think Ben should not *have the operation no matter what the probabilities.*

____The chances are 9 in 10 that the operation will be a success.

____The chances are 7 in 10 that the operation will be a success.

____The chances are 5 in 10 that the operation will be a success.

____The chances are 3 in 10 that the operation will be a success.

____The chances are 1 in 10 that the operation will be a success.

2. Don is the captain of Alpha College's football team. Alpha College is playing its traditional rival, Beta College, in the final game of the season. The game is in its final seconds, and Don's team, Alpha College, is losing. Alpha has time to run one more play. Don, as captain, must decide if it would be best to settle for a tie score with a play that would be almost certain to work or, on the other hand, should he try a more complicated and risky play that could bring victory if it succeeded, but defeat if it did not.

Imagine you are advising Don. The following lists several probabilities or odds that the risky play will work. Check the *lowest probability* that you would consider acceptable for the risky play to be attempted.

____Place a check here if you think Don should not *attempt the risky play no matter what the probabilities are.*

____The chances are 9 in 10 that the risky play will work.

____The chances are 7 in 10 that the risky play will work.

____The chances are 5 in 10 that the risky play will work.

____The chances are 3 in 10 that the risky play will work.

____The chances are 1 in 10 that the risky play will work.

3. Kim is a successful businesswoman who has participated in a number of civic activities of considerable value to the community. Kim has been approached by the leaders of her political party as a possible congressional candidate in the next election. Kim's party is a minority in the district, although the party has won occasional elections in the past. Kim would like to hold political office, but to do so would involve a financial sacrifice because the party has insufficient campaign funds. She would also have to endure the attacks of her political opponents in a hot campaign.

Imagine you are advising Kim. The following lists several probabilities or odds of Kim's winning the election in her district. Check the *lowest probability* that you would consider acceptable to make it worthwhile for Kim to run for political office.

____*Place a check here if you think Kim should* not *run for political office no matter what the probabilities are.*

____*The chances are 9 in 10 that Kim would win the election.*

____*The chances are 7 in 10 that Kim would win the election.*

____*The chances are 5 in 10 that Kim would win the election.*

____*The chances are 3 in 10 that Kim would win the election.*

____*The chances are 1 in 10 that Kim would win the election.*

4. Laura, a 30-year-old research physicist, has been given a five-year appointment by a major university laboratory. As she contemplates the next five years, she realizes she might work on a difficult long-term problem which, if a solution could be found, would resolve basic scientific issues in the field and bring high scientific honors. If no solution were found, however, Laura would have little to show for her five years in the laboratory, and this would make it hard for her to get a good job afterward. On the other hand, she could, as most of her professional associates

are doing, work on a series of short-term problems where solutions would be easier to find, but where the problems are of lesser scientific importance.

Imagine you are advising Laura. The following lists several probabilities or odds that a solution would be found to the difficult long-term problem that Laura has in mind. Check the *lowest probability* that you would consider acceptable to make it worthwhile for Laura to work on the more difficult long-term problem.

___*Place a check here if you think Laura should not choose the long-term difficult problem, no matter what the probabilities.*

___*The chances are 1 in 10 that Laura would solve the long-term problem.*

___*The chances are 3 in 10 that Laura would solve the long-term problem.*

___*The chances are 5 in 10 that Laura would solve the long-term problem.*

___*The chances are 7 in 10 that Laura would solve the long-term problem.*

___*The chances are 9 in 10 that Laura would solve the long-term problem.*

How to Score

This series of situations is based on a longer questionnaire. As such, your results are meant to indicate a general orientation toward risk rather than to act as a precise measure. To calculate your risk-taking score, add up the chances you were willing to take and divide by 4. (For any of the situations in which you would not take the risk regardless of the probabilities, give yourself a 10.)

What Your Score Means

The lower your number, the more risk taking you are. For comparative purposes, a risk-index score of lower than 4.0 suggests you have a relatively high-risk profile. Scores of 7.0 or higher suggest risk aversion.

Understanding Risk Taking

People differ in their willingness to take chances. High risk takers, for instance, are more likely than their low-risk counterparts to pursue entrepreneurial business opportunities or to engage in sports like rock climbing and hang gliding.

An understanding of risk is important for decision makers because it helps shape the appeal of decision alternatives. When you evaluate decisions, alternatives will differ in their degree of risk. Low-risk seekers are likely to identify, value, and choose alternatives that have low chances for failure. Right or wrong, that often means alternatives that contain minimal change from the status quo. High risk takers, on the other hand, are more likely to identify, value, and choose alternatives that are unique and that have a greater chance of failing.

Who Controls Your Destiny?

For each of the following 10 statements, select the choice (a or b) with which you agree more.[1]

1. a. *Making a lot of money is largely a matter of getting the right breaks.*

   b. *Promotions are earned through hard work and persistence.*

2. a. *There was a direct connection between how hard I studied in school and the grades I got.*

   b. *Many times, the reactions of my teachers in school seemed haphazard to me.*

3. a. *The number of divorces indicates that more and more people are not trying to make their marriages work.*

   b. *Marriage is largely a gamble.*

4. a. *It's silly to think that one can really change another person's basic attitudes.*

   b. *When I am right, I can convince others.*

5. a. *Getting promoted is really a matter of being a little luckier than the next person.*

b. *In our society, a person's future earning power is dependent upon his or her ability.*

6. a. *If one knows how to deal with people, they are really quite easily led.*

   b. *I have little influence over the way other people behave.*

7. a. *The grades I made in school were the result of my own efforts; luck had little or nothing to do with it.*

   b. *Sometimes I felt that I had little to do with the grades I got.*

8. a. *People like me can change the course of world affairs if we make ourselves heard.*

   b. *It is only wishful thinking to believe that one can readily influence what happens in our society.*

9. a. *A great deal that happens to me is probably a matter of chance.*

   b. *I am the master of my fate.*

10. a. *Getting along with people is a skill that must be practiced.*

    b. *It's almost impossible to figure out how to please some people.*

How to Score

Give yourself 1 point for each of the following selections: 1b, 2a, 3a, 4b, 5b, 6a, 7a, 8a, 9b, and 10a. Now add up your total of points.

Your score can be interpreted as follows:

8–10 = High internal locus of control

6–7 = Moderate internal locus of control

5 = Mixed

3–4 = Moderate external locus of control

1–2 = High external locus of control

What Your Score Means

Some people believe that they're masters of their own fate. Other people see themselves as pawns of fate, believing that what happens to them in their lives is due to luck or chance. The first type—who believe that they control their destinies—have an *internal* locus of control. The latter type—who see their lives as being controlled by outside forces—have an *external* locus of control.[2]

Your locus of control score can provide you with insights into how well you accept blame for your actions. It can also suggest the degree of importance you place on improving your decision-making skills. People with a high external locus of control, for instance, tend to see themselves as relatively powerless in influencing their life. As such, they're less concerned with developing strong decision-making skills because they don't believe that their choices have much effect on their life outcomes. In contrast, high internals tend to be proactive. They sincerely believe that they can control their destiny. Because they believe that the choices they make really matter, they tend to be more highly motivated to learn better decision-making techniques.

Understanding Locus of Control

People with very high internal scores may be guilty of believing the world is more controllable than it really is. People with very high external scores may be too quick to assume that they are merely a pawn in life's game. Neither of these extreme positions is healthy. We *can* control a good part of our life, but there will always be surprises that no amount of planning or good judgment could have anticipated. For high externals, my message is to realize that you have options, that your decisions do make a difference, and that learning good decision-making skills can put you more in control of your life.

Do You Procrastinate?

The following lists a variety of thoughts that sometimes pop into people's heads. Read each thought and indicate how frequently, if at all, you think the thought has occurred to you during the past two weeks.[1]

Score your responses using the following five-point scale:

0 = Not at all

1 = Sometimes

2 = Moderately often

3 = Often

4 = All of the time

	0	1	2	3	4
1. Why can't I do what I *should* be doing.	—	—	—	—	—
2. I need to start earlier.	—	—	—	—	—
3. I should be more responsible.	—	—	—	—	—
4. No matter how much I try, I still put things off.	—	—	—	—	—

33

	0	1	2	3	4
5. Why can't I just get started.	—	—	—	—	—
6. I know I'm behind but I can catch up.	—	—	—	—	—
7. I'm letting myself down.	—	—	—	—	—
8. This is not how I want to be.	—	—	—	—	—
9. It would be great if everything in my life were done on time.	—	—	—	—	—
10. I'm such a procrastinator, I'll never reach my goals.	—	—	—	—	—
11. I need deadlines to get me going.	—	—	—	—	—
12. Why can't I finish things that I start.	—	—	—	—	—
13. Why didn't I start earlier.	—	—	—	—	—

How to Score

Add up your individual responses for the 13 items. Your score will fall somewhere between 0 and 52. The higher your score, the more you're prone to procrastinate.

What Your Score Means

Scores of 13 or less suggest you don't delay decisions or life activities. Scores of 35 or higher, on the other hand, indicate you may be prone to postpone doing things and experience frustrations over actions not taken.

Understanding Procrastination

Procrastination is a tendency to postpone, delay, or avoid performing tasks or making decisions.[2] In some situations, procrastination can be positive. For instance, if you lack sufficient information to make an informed decision, if other pressing matters with higher priorities demand attention, or if the consequences of a decision are so weighty that more deliberation is needed, procrastination is likely to reduce the chances of making a bad decision.[3] However, chronic procrastination can lead to lost opportunities, regrets, and other negative outcomes.

As I elaborate on in Chapter 13, high procrastinators are likely to have trouble making minor decisions ("I know I should clean out my closets but . . .") as well as major decisions ("I want to get married, but I'm not sure if now is the right time"). For many people, procrastination consistently hinders them from taking actions and changing things in their lives, but low scores on this test also may indicate problems. Low procrastinators often act prematurely and later regret their actions. A little procrastination, particularly on important decisions, may save you a lot of money and aggravation.

Are You Impulsive?

The following contains 30 statements. Indicate the degree to which they describe you by circling the appropriate number.[1]

	Never/ Rarely	Occasionally	Often	Most Always/ Always
1. I plan tasks carefully.	4	3	2	1
2. I do things without thinking.	1	2	3	4
3. I make up my mind quickly.	1	2	3	4
4. I am happy-go-lucky.	1	2	3	4
5. I don't "pay attention."	1	2	3	4
6. I have "racing" thoughts.	1	2	3	4
7. I plan trips well ahead of time.	4	3	2	1
8. I am self-controlled.	4	3	2	1
9. I concentrate easily.	4	3	2	1
10. I save regularly.	4	3	2	1
11. I "squirm" at plays or lectures.	1	2	3	4
12. I am a careful thinker.	4	3	2	1
13. I plan for job security.	4	3	2	1
14. I say things without thinking.	1	2	3	4

	Never/ Rarely	Occasionally	Often	Most Always/ Always
15. I like to think about complex problems.	4	3	2	1
16. I change jobs.	1	2	3	4
17. I act "on impulse."	1	2	3	4
18. I get easily bored when solving thought problems.	1	2	3	4
19. I act on the spur of the moment.	1	2	3	4
20. I am a steady thinker.	4	3	2	1
21. I change residences.	1	2	3	4
22. I buy things on impulse.	1	2	3	4
23. I can only think about one problem at a time.	1	2	3	4
24. I change hobbies.	1	2	3	4
25. I spend or charge more than I earn.	1	2	3	4
26. I often have extraneous thoughts when thinking.	1	2	3	4
27. I am more interested in the present than the future.	1	2	3	4
28. I am restless at the theatre or lectures.	1	2	3	4
29. I like puzzles.	4	3	2	1
30. I don't "pay attention."	4	3	2	1

How to Score

Add up your circled responses to the 30 items. Your score will fall somewhere between 30 and 120. The higher your score, the higher your level of impulsiveness.

Understanding Impulsiveness

An impulsive personality is made up of three subtraits.[2] The first measures your ability to focus on the task at hand and to control racing thoughts. The second assesses your tendency to act on the spur of the moment. And the third measures your ability to think ahead and to enjoy challenging mental tasks. Together, these three subtraits provide a fairly consistent measure of impulsiveness.

Like procrastination, impulsiveness in some situations can be positive. For minor decisions that have minimal long-term consequences, being able to decide quickly minimizes stress and can make life easier. However, for major decisions that influence the trajectory of your life path, impulsiveness can lead to inconsistent and poor-quality decisions.

What Does Your Score Mean?

As noted, the higher your score, the more impulsive you are. So what's *high*? A study comparing college students, psychiatric patients with substance-abuse problems, and prison inmates can help us answer that question.[3] It seems reasonable to expect substance-abuse patients and prisoners to score higher than normal college students because such individuals are more likely to have impulse-control problems. And that's what the study found. The average score by the college students was 64. The substance-abuse patients averaged 69, and the prisoners scored just over 76. Based on these results, I suggest that scores lower than 60 indicate substantial control over your impulses, and scores more than 70 indicate a relatively high tendency toward impulsive action.

Your score can help you size up how prone you might be toward making decisions too quickly or if you have difficulty delaying desire for instant gratification. It's also more difficult for people with a high impulsive tendency to set goals and to stay focused on those goals.

Can You Control Your Emotions?

The following lists some of the reactions people have to certain feelings or emotions. Read each one and indicate how it describes the way you *generally* react. Indicate your answer by circling the appropriate number. [1]

	Almost Always	Frequently	Occasionally	Almost Never
When I feel angry:				
1. I keep quiet.	4	3	2	1
2. I refuse to argue or say anything.	4	3	2	1
3. I bottle it up.	4	3	2	1
4. I say what I feel.	1	2	3	4
5. I avoid making a scene.	4	3	2	1
6. I smother my feelings.	4	3	2	1
7. I hide my annoyance.	4	3	2	1
When I feel depressed:				
8. I refuse to say anything about it.	4	3	2	1
9. I hide my unhappiness.	4	3	2	1
10. I put on a bold face.	4	3	2	1

41

	Almost Always	Frequently	Occasionally	Almost Never
11. I keep quiet.	4	3	2	1
12. I let others see how I feel.	1	2	3	4
13. I smother my feelings.	4	3	2	1
14. I bottle it up.	4	3	2	1

When I feel anxious:

	Almost Always	Frequently	Occasionally	Almost Never
15. I let others see how I feel.	1	2	3	4
16. I keep quiet.	4	3	2	1
17. I refuse to say anything about it.	4	3	2	1
18. I tell others all about it.	1	2	3	4
19. I say what I feel.	1	2	3	4
20. I bottle it up.	4	3	2	1
21. I smother my feelings.	4	3	2	1

How to Score

Add up the numbers you circled. Your score will fall somewhere between 21 and 84. The higher your score, the greater control you exhibit over your emotions.

What Your Score Means

Your score reflects your response to three emotions: anger, depression, and anxiety. Although this doesn't cover every emotion you're likely to experience, your score provides important insights into how your feelings might influence how you make decisions.

High scores (approximately 50 or higher) suggest you have relatively strong control over your emotions. Low scores (approximately 40 or less) indicate that your emotions can sometimes get the best of you. For instance, in times of crisis or stress, you may show occasional outbursts and lose your cool. When you're calm, it's easier to be clear thinking and rational, which is more likely to lead to making better choices. However, after a decision is made, strong emotional commitment becomes a plus because it frequently increases the likelihood that the decision will be carried out. So emotions often provide the motivation to translate decision choices into action. However, for the most part, you're likely to make better decisions when you're calm and have your emotions under control.

Understanding Emotions

Emotions are intense feelings that are directed toward someone or something. I express emotions when I'm angry at my landlord, fearful of losing my job, or happy about my daughter's good grades in school.

The rational model of decision making downplays the role of anxiety, fear, frustration, happiness, envy, and similar emotions. Yet it's naïve to assume that decision choices aren't influenced by our feelings at a particular moment. Given the same objective data, we should expect that people may make different choices when they're angry and stressed-out than when they're calm and collected. And some people are much more likely to let their immediate emotions shape their decision choices than are others. Negative emotions, for instance, can result in a limited search for new alternatives, a less vigilant use of information, or the desire to make a decision too quickly.

Are You Overconfident?

For each of the following 10 items, provide a low and high guess so that you are 90 percent sure the correct answer falls between the two guesses. Your challenge is to be neither too narrow nor too wide.[1]

	90% Confidence Range	
	Low	**High**
1. Martin Luther King Jr.'s age at death	_____	_____
2. Length of the Nile River	_____	_____
3. Number of countries that are full members of OPEC	_____	_____
4. Number of books in the Old Testament	_____	_____
5. Diameter of the moon in miles	_____	_____
6. Weight of an empty Boeing 747 (in pounds)	_____	_____
7. Year in which Wolfgang Amadeus Mozart was born	_____	_____
8. Gestation period (in days) of an Asian elephant	_____	_____
9. Air distance from London to Tokyo	_____	_____

| | **90% Confidence Range** | |
| | **Low** | **High** |

10. Deepest known point in the ocean (in feet)   _____   _____

How to Score

The correct answers to this quiz are as follows: (1) 39 years; (2) 4,187 miles; (3) 13 countries as of 2003; (4) 39 books; (5) 2,160 miles; (6) 390,000 pounds; (7) 1756; (8) 645 days; (9) 5,959 miles; (10) 36,198 feet.

If you successfully met the challenge—that is, achieved 90 percent confidence—you should have 10 percent misses. That converts to getting nine of the above estimates correct.

Did you get more than one question wrong? If you did, you're not alone. This test was administered to more than 1,000 people and *less than one percent of the respondents got nine or more items correct*. Most people missed four to seven of the answers. Similar trivia tests taken by Americans, Asians, and Europeans also found that most people are overconfident— missing four to seven questions out of 10.[2]

What Your Score Means

The 10 trivia questions were not designed to test how much you know about obscure facts. Rather, they were designed to illustrate how overconfident most of us are in saying that we know what we don't know.

Depending upon the degree to which you might suffer from overconfidence, the quality of your decision process will suffer. The lower the number of items that you got right, the more you tend to exhibit overconfidence. And this can show itself in several ways when you make decisions. It can lead you to seek support for your initial views on a problem and to ignore disconfirming evidence. It can restrict the number of alternatives you feel you need to develop. And it can close your mind to analyzing your alternatives thoroughly.

Understanding Overconfidence

As I elaborate on in Chapter 12, most of us suffer from overconfidence when we make estimates. That is, we tend to be more confident about what we know than we should be. "Good decision making requires not only knowing the facts, but understanding the limits of your knowledge." [3]

Chapter Eleven

Understanding Your Personality Profile

I'm not much, baby—but I'm all I've got.

—J. Lair

Holly and Chris have been married for five years. They argue frequently over almost everything. One of their "favorite" topics is how the other makes decisions. Holly is slow and deliberate. She doesn't like to rush into anything without considering her options. Even for a decision as trivial as ordering a meal in a restaurant, Holly takes her time and carefully looks over the entire menu. Chris, on the other hand, seems to process information at breakneck speed. He rarely spends a lot of time on a decision. He quickly sizes up a situation, rapidly considers his options, and then makes his choice. When things don't work out as he planned, he rarely complains. He neither obsesses on choices he has to make nor on his past mistakes.

Much of the differences in how Holly and Chris go about making judgments and choices can be explained by the differences in their personalities. Looking back on the tests in Chapters 4 through 10, some of the couple's scores explain a lot. Chris, for instance, rated much higher than Holly on intuition. Chris is comfortable going with his "gut feelings" while Holly prefers a more slow, deliberate, and rational approach. Chris

49

also scored much higher on risk taking than Holly. He's more willing to take chances and live with the consequences. And Chris also scored a lot lower than Holly on the procrastination test.

Like Holly and Chris, the way we approach decisions is strongly affected by our personalities. Although our personalities are complex, with numerous components, the tests you took in Chapters 4 through 10 provide a fairly good profile of how you tend to approach decision situations.

Begin by looking at your locus of control score (Chapter 6). If you have a high external locus, you tend to see yourself as relatively powerless in shaping your future. As such, you're not likely to have much confidence that learning better decision skills will improve your life. Hopefully, the evidence, examples, and suggestions presented in coming chapters can help you to see otherwise. Your procrastination and impulsiveness scores (Chapters 7 and 8) indicate how you tend to react when you see a problem. These scores indicate whether you prefer to solve problems quickly, wait a bit, or try to avoid taking action. Once you see a problem, do you try to solve it by using your brain or your gut? Do you rely on facts and logic or your personal values and intuition? Your decision style score (Chapter 4) can help answer that. And do you prefer safe options, or are you willing to chance failing? Your risk-taking score (Chapter 5) will provide you with insights. Finally, you're more likely to make better decisions if you can control your emotions (Chapter 9) and limit tendencies toward overconfidence (Chapter 10).

Your personality does *impact the choices you make.*

You should treat this personality information as insight into your tendencies and avoid making judgments as to whether those tendencies are good or bad. All of us have some traits that bias our decision making. Additionally, don't look at your test results in isolation.

Personality traits are not rigid predictors. You have to look at each in the context of various situations. You may, for instance, exhibit strong procrastinating tendencies when it comes to scheduling appointments with your dentist for a checkup. On the other hand, your work projects may always be completed on time. Situational differences, therefore, can override your personality tendencies.

At this point, you need to remember that (1) your personality *does* impact the choices you make, (2) a personality characteristic that hinders you in one instance can be an asset in another, (3) situational factors can strengthen or weaken the influence of personality traits, and (4) awareness of your personality tendencies is the first step toward making adjustments that can limit the negative impact those tendencies might create.

Decision Tips

- Your personality influences how you approach decision situations.

- You need to know your major personality tendencies.

- A personality trait that hinders you in one instance can be an asset in another.

Common Biases and Errors That Most of Us Make (and How to Overcome Them)

How Can You Be So Darn Sure About That? Coping with Overconfidence

It's not what we don't know that gives us trouble,
it's what we know that ain't so.

—J. Billings

You can't overestimate people's confidence in their opinions. Even experts in their field often think they know more than they do. A few famous quotes illustrate just how off the mark even the "best and the brightest" can be:

"Stocks have reached what looks like a permanently high plateau." (Irving Fisher, Yale University economist in 1929, just before the market crash and the Great Depression)

"No matter what happens, the U.S. Navy is not going to be caught napping." (U.S. Secretary of the Navy, December 4, 1941, three days before the surprise attack on Pearl Harbor)

"We don't like their sound and guitar music is on the way out." (A Decca Recording Company executive explaining, in 1962, why he rejected signing the Beatles)

"There is no reason anyone would want a computer in their home." (Ken Olson, founder of Digital Equipment Co., in 1977).

It's probably correct to say that "no problem in judgment and decision making is more prevalent and more potentially catastrophic than overconfidence."[1] Almost all of us suffer from it. Look back on your answers to the overconfidence test in Chapter 10. Did you score less than 9 out of 10? If so, join the overconfidence club.

As pointed out in Chapter 10, when we're given factual questions and asked to judge the probability that our answers are correct, we tend to be far too optimistic. We can extend this to say that, in general, people hold unrealistically positive views of themselves and their performance.

> "New entrepreneurs wildly overestimate the chances that their enterprises will succeed, business planners grossly underestimate project completion times, and people generally believe that they will be happier, more confident, more hardworking, and less lonely in the future than their peers."[2]

Studies have found that, when people say they're 65 to 70 percent confident that they're right, they were actually correct only about 50 percent of the time.[3] And when they say they're 100 percent sure, they tended to only be 70 to 85 percent correct.[4]

We seem to be particularly vulnerable to overconfidence when we're making self-evaluations. A survey of a million high school seniors found that they *all* thought they were above average in their ability to get along with others, 60 percent considered themselves to be in the top 10 percent, and a full 25 percent thought they were in the top one percent![5] Most of us also suffer from thinking we're better than we actually are at performing tasks. For instance, we tend to have an inflated view of our work performance. Statistically speaking, half of all employees must be below-average performers. However, the evidence indicates that the average employee's estimate of his or her own performance level generally falls around the 75th percentile.[6] We additionally tend to believe that our futures will prove to be better than those of others.[7]

Our overconfidence can really play havoc when it comes to our investment decisions.[8] It leads us to the erroneous belief that we can pick mutual funds or stocks that will outperform the market.[9] During the heyday of day-trading in the late 1990s, millions of people lost billions of dollars because they were convinced they could outwit the market averages.

This optimism tendency doesn't apply to all people or situations equally. It's most likely to surface when confidence is extremely high or accurate judgments are difficult to make.[10] So be on guard when someone tells you he or she's 95 or 100 percent sure of anything!

When people say they're 100 percent sure that they're right, they tend to only be 70 to 85 percent correct.

Additionally, those individuals whose intellectual and interpersonal abilities are *weakest* are most likely to overestimate their performance and ability.[11] Apparently, as we become more knowledgeable about an issue, we're less likely to display overconfidence.[12] So overconfidence is most likely to surface when considering issues and problems that are outside our area of expertise. But, as the opening quotes in this chapter illustrate, even experts can suffer from overconfidence.

Why do we tend to be overconfident? A number of influences can lead us in this direction.[13] First is the illusion of superiority. We tend to have both unrealistically positive views of ourselves and to be unrealistic about our future relative to others. Second is the naïve belief that we can control random events. We want to believe we're in full control of our destiny, and strong confidence in our decision-making ability reinforces this. Third is our limited ability to imagine all the ways that events can unfold. We become overconfident because we fail to realize how many ways we can be wrong. Fourth is our tendency to seek information that confirms what we already believe. We often start our search for alternatives with an initial favorite and then focus on finding information that supports this favorite rather than look for disconfirming evidence. And finally, we're not very good at objectively appraising our past decision record. We selectively assess our past decisions by remembering our successes and forgetting our failures. This reinforces our belief that we're better at predicting the future than we really are.

Confidence is important for success in life, and nothing in this chapter should discourage you from believing in yourself or your ability to make good choices. Unfounded overconfidence, however, can get you into trouble. So what can you do to limit this malady?[14] Begin by recognizing that you're likely to be overconfident and look for signs of that overconfidence. Also, search hard for disconfirming evidence and look for reasons why your prediction might be wrong. The Chief Executive Officer of Houston-based ATP Oil & Gas, for instance, uses this approach when interviewing job candidates. "If I like the person immediately, I will try to think of all the reasons why that individual won't work out at the company. However, if I am quick to form a judgment that the person probably won't work out at ATP, I try to find every way to change my mind—to find things about the person that I know are going to work out here. And by taking the reverse position from my immediate instincts, frequently I will learn things that I otherwise would never know."[15]

If you have trouble with this process, sometimes asking others to offer counterarguments can help you to better see flaws in your position. Unconstrained by your biases, others often can see things you can't. Finally, you should adjust your confidence awareness to reflect your level of expertise on an issue. You're most likely to be overconfident when considering areas outside of your expertise. For most of us, this should put us on alert not to be too cocky about our bargaining skills when making a major purchase--like buying a new car--or trying to get the best deal on an apartment rental. Our adversaries in these cases are typically professional negotiators, and we're not. These are instances where overconfidence is likely to lead us to an exaggerated belief about our chances of success.

Decision Tips

- Recognize your tendency to be overconfident.

- Be especially alert to overconfidence when considering issues outside your expertise.

- Look for reasons why your predictions or answers might be wrong.

Never Do Today That Which You Can Do Tomorrow: The Inertia Bias

Even if you're on the right track,
you'll get run over if you just sit there.

—W. Rogers

Chuck Randall was a smart guy. He had a Ph.D. in business and was a professor at a major state university. When he saw his technology-laden retirement funds drop 20 percent between March and July 2000, he realized the market could go a lot lower. He thought he probably should get out of high-tech stocks, but that July turned to August and the months went by. By summer of 2002, Chuck hadn't sold a single share, but his procrastination had cost him dearly. Between March 2000 and July 2002, his portfolio had lost more than 75 percent of its value.

Look back at Chapter 7. Are you a procrastinator? Do you have a tendency to postpone, delay, or avoid performing tasks or making decisions?[1] We all can get caught up in the inertia bias, but some of us suffer this malady much more than others. In this chapter, I look at why we often have trouble making a decision and present several techniques we can practice that can help us overcome this tendency.

Procrastination is a general disposition to postpone doing things. We all suffer from it on occasion: We don't want to begin our Christmas shopping; we avoid going to the dentist; we put off balancing our checkbook. Chronic indecision, when it relates to isolated minor issues, rarely has any long-term effects on your life. It's when this chronic state involves ongoing daily activities (meeting work deadlines, fulfilling family obligations) or major issues in your life (career choices, marriage, developing a retirement program) that it becomes debilitating. Evidence indicates, for instance, that chronically indecisive people become depressed about the circumstances of their lives and often feel trapped because they don't know how to change.[2]

What causes procrastination? There's no simple answer to this question. Numerous factors have been suggested:

- Fragile self-esteem

- Fear of making mistakes

- Being a perfectionist

- Desire to maintain control

- Lack of motivation

- Poor organization

- Competing claims on time[3]

Most of the evidence, however, indicates that the primary cause of procrastination is conflict.[4]

> When one option is better than another in all essential respects, there is no conflict and choice is easy. However, when each option has significant advantages and disadvantages, people often experience conflict that makes choice aversive and compels them to delay decision and seek additional information or options.[5]

Your procrastination tendencies are minimized when you have to make decisions where there is only one obvious option or your options can be clearly rank-ordered by preferences. However, when you're faced with multiple options that are all too similar, the tendency is to avoid making a choice and to continue gathering more information.[6] This would be true even if your options contain one or more satisfactory alternatives. It's also irrelevant if choices appear similar when they're really not. This is because we act on perceptions rather than reality. If you perceive your options as all being basically alike, you can delay making a choice and can continue indefinitely to search for more information or new alternatives.

Note that in the rational decision process (see Chapters 2 and 3), conflicts aren't a problem. It's assumed that decision makers can objectively rate and preference-rank all alternatives. In the real world, however, our options are rarely so easy to differentiate. So we experience conflict.

In addition to conflict, the task itself can be a major source of procrastination.[7] We typically try to avoid tasks or decisions that we find unpleasant. We know we should see the dentist twice a year, but we put off making an appointment. Or we postpone following up on the resume we sent out in response to a job ad for fear of rejection. That long list

Chronically indecisive people become depressed about the circumstances of their lives and often feel trapped because they don't know how to change.

of things we say we want to do, but are pretty good at postponing—going on a diet, quitting smoking, beginning a regular workout program, paying off our credit cards—can largely be explained as due to the perception that these are all unappealing tasks, where the immediate pain seems greater than any long-term benefits.

If you tend to be a procrastinator, are you compelled to forever carry this burden? Although it's difficult to overcome procrastination, there are a couple of things you can do. For minor decisions, it's OK to tell yourself "don't worry about it; just make a choice." For example, selecting a meal from a restaurant menu, deciding what jacket to wear today, or choosing what movie to see tonight are not usually worth worrying over. With decisions of this type, the cost for making a "wrong" choice is typically minimal.[8] For major decisions, consider imposing voluntary constraints on yourself.[9] For instance, you can impose deadlines that, if missed, would be embarrassing or costly. This works best when your deadline is voiced publicly. When I was contemplating taking early retirement from my university position, I began publicly announcing my intention 18 months ahead of time. This public commitment helped me to make the final decision by making it embarrassing for me to delay it. Here's another example of imposing a voluntary constraint: If you're trying to lose weight, you can go to a restaurant that offers only soups and salads rather than, say, the Cheesecake Factory—thus eliminating many high-calorie temptations.

Decision Tips

- Your procrastination score indicates a general tendency.
- For minor decisions, just make a choice.
- For major decisions, consider imposing voluntary constraints on yourself.

I Want It, and I Want it NOW!
The Immediate Gratification Bias

Patience doesn't always help,
but impatience never does.
—*Anonymous*

Sheri Weiner grew up in relative affluence. She got a car when she turned 16. Her dad gave her a credit card for her 17th birthday. Her folks paid her college tuition and sent her a check each month to cover her additional college expenses. Sheri never really grasped concepts like budgets, saving money, or delaying immediate gratification. When she saw something she wanted, she bought it.

Sheri is now 25. She has a full-time job, a nicely furnished apartment, a well-stocked wardrobe closet, and a huge stack of bills. A week doesn't go by that she doesn't get a call from one of her creditors asking for money. When I asked Sheri how much she owed, she thought for a moment and then said, "I have to admit, I'm not really sure. If you count all my credit cards, I'd guess about $15,000." Sheri guessed wrong! Finally fed up with the constant hassles from collection agencies, she went to a bill-consolidation service. They carefully tallied up her credit card debts—all $37,000 of them! Moreover, they showed Sheri that her $400 minimum monthly payment on those cards wasn't even covering the $550 a month she was accumulating in interest. Sheri was dumbfounded. How did she get herself into this mess?

Sheri is not unique. More than 65 percent of U.S. households pay interest on credit card balances.[1] And, in 2001, that average balance was $7,034.[2] "Buy now. Pay later!" has become the mantra of consumers in much of the industrialized world. For many people, it's very hard to delay immediate gratification. Interestingly, this behavior is essentially the opposite of procrastination. Both are self-control problems, but one relates to the preference for inertia while the other reflects a present-biased preference. In addition, both behaviors are one-part personality and one-part situational. Look back at your results for impulsiveness in Chapter 8. If you scored more than 70 on that test, you are likely to have difficulty in postponing immediate gratification. As you'll see, there are rewards and costs that lead all of us toward preferring the immediate over the long-term. Yet some people have become quite proficient at learning how to control the immediate gratification bias.

Why is it so hard to diet, quit smoking, or avoid credit card debt? Each comes with an immediate reward, and each delays its costs to some nebulous future.

As human beings, we suffer from the tendency to want to grab for immediate rewards and to avoid immediate costs.[3] If it feels good, we want to do it now. If it implies pain, we want to postpone it. Why is it hard to diet, quit smoking, or avoid credit card debt? Each comes with an immediate reward—tasty food, an enjoyable cigarette, or an immediate purchase—and each delays its costs to some nebulous future.

In recent years, the concept of *emotional intelligence (EI)* has gotten a great deal of attention.[4] The evidence indicates that people with strong EI have superior coping skills and are better able to deal well with life's pressures and stress. One element of this concept that interests us is that studies show people with strong EI have the ability to delay gratification. For instance, in one study, four-year olds were given two choices. They could receive one marshmallow immediately or wait a few minutes and receive two. In a follow-up 10 years later, the study found that the kids who could delay gratification were less easily frustrated, less stubborn, more popular, more confident, better able to handle stress, and generally had less trouble dealing with life than those who sought instant gratification. This makes a pretty strong case for the value of EI and the ability to delay immediate gratification.

Let's spend a moment returning to the situational aspects of delayed gratification. Regardless of our personality disposition, activities that provide immediate rewards with delayed costs inherently encourage us to "live for the moment." Unfortunately, our lives are filled with decisions that require a longer-term perspective, and many of these decisions are very important. For instance, the decision to drop out of college and go to work provides immediate rewards—a regular paycheck and the cessation of unpleasant tasks like attending classes, studying, and taking exams. Meanwhile, the payoff from getting that college degree remains uncertain. It's often difficult for an 18-year-old to see four years or more into the future. Similarly, putting money away each month for retirement requires us to forego spending today in hope that our money will grow and that we'll be alive to enjoy it. Notice that both of these situations not only have delayed payoffs from postponing immediate gratification, but that the payoffs are uncertain.

One of the reasons many of us lack patience and a long-term perspective is that the further a payoff lies into the future, the less we tend to value it. To many an 18-year-old, a great job in 20 years (which requires a college degree) or a comfortable retirement in 40 years (because we began saving early) seems a long way away, and hence will be heavily discounted. We know what a dollar will buy today, but we don't know its value in 10 or 20 years. This was driven home to me by a professor/friend of mine, who was explaining why he stopped writing books and focused his time on consulting. "I do a consulting job, and I'm paid a fixed and predictable sum within a few weeks of completing the assignment. I write a book, and I have to wait a year or two for it to be published and to get a royalty check. And then the check could be for $20,000 or $100. I love writing, but consulting provides me with an immediate and known reward."

If you want to overcome the temptations of immediate gratification, you can do a couple of things. First, set long-term goals and review them regularly. This can help you focus on the longer term and help you to justify making decisions whose payoffs may be far into the future. If you don't know where you want to be in 10 or 20 years, it's easier to discount your future and live for the moment. Second, pay attention to both rewards *and costs*. Our natural tendency is to inflate immediate rewards and underplay future costs. For important decisions, carefully consider future costs. For instance, think about what it would be like to be broke in your old age. Also, look around for examples of people who didn't plan for their future and now suffer the consequences. If you're having trouble keeping your credit card spending in control, talk with a few people whose credit card debts led them to bankruptcy. Listen as they describe the anguish and embarrassment they've had to suffer.

Decision Tips

- Know your personality tendencies toward immediate gratification.
- Set long-term goals and review them regularly.
- Fully consider future costs.

Where You End Up Depends on Where You Start: The Anchoring Effect

*The more you ask for,
the more you get.*

—Anonymous

Brian and Rhonda had been looking for a home for several months. Then they came across the perfect place. The seller was asking $295,000 for it. Brian, always the smart negotiator, began doing his homework. He got a report listing all recent home sales in the area. He found ones that were similar to the one he wanted. He compared them on lot size, number of rooms, square footage, quality of construction, age, condition, and similar factors. After this careful analysis, Brian concluded that the fair market value for this house was $255,000. Now came the challenge. If Brian allowed the seller to focus on the $295,000 asking price, Brian was on the defensive. He would have to explain why he was offering $40,000 less. However, if Brian could get the seller to focus on Brian's $255,000 offer—that is, to get the seller to justify why the house *isn't* correctly priced at $255,000 when compared with other recent sales—he'd have a much better chance of buying the house for something close to $255,000. In essence, Brian was attempting to switch the point of negotiation from the asking price to his offer price.

Brian understood the anchoring effect. He realized that the initial starting point of a negotiation plays a major part in determining the final outcome. In this chapter, you'll see how the anchoring effect shapes a number of decisions—from negotiations to jury verdicts—and what you can do to lessen its influence.

The *anchoring effect* is a tendency to fixate on initial information as a starting point. Once set, we then fail to adequately adjust for subsequent information.[1] Why does this occur? Our mind appears to give a disproportionate amount of emphasis to the first information it receives. So initial impressions, ideas, prices, and estimates carry undue weight relative to information received later.[2]

Anchors are widely used by people in the persuasion professions such as advertisers, politicians, real estate agents, and lawyers. For instance, in a mock jury trial, one set of jurors was asked by the plaintiff's attorney to make an award in the range of $15 million to $50 million. Another set of jurors was asked for an award in the range of $50 million to $150 million. Consistent with the anchoring effect, the median awards were $15 million versus $50 million in the two conditions.[3]

Negotiations aren't limited to the persuasion professions, however. All of us are involved in bargaining. We buy a new car. We buy or sell a home or business. We create a prenuptial contract or negotiate a starting salary. And any time a negotiation takes place, so does anchoring. As soon as someone states a number, your ability to objectively ignore that number has been compromised. For instance, when a prospective employer asks how much you were making in your prior job, your answer typically anchors the employer's offer. Most of us understand this and upwardly "adjust" our previous salary in the hope that it will encourage our new employer to offer us more.

Let's look again at home prices because, for most us, buying or selling a home is one of the biggest financial decisions we make. The evidence indicates that not only is the typical buyer anchored by a property's initial price, so are the "experts."[4] An experiment with experienced real estate agents in Tucson, Arizona, illustrates this point. The agents were given a detailed 10-page packet describing a number of homes and then taken on a tour of these properties. The packet contained standard Multiple Listing Service listing sheets, recent housing sales data for the city and the neighborhoods, and data about current homes for sale on the market. The agents were then asked to assess "fair market values" and to predict selling prices for these homes. The catch in this experiment was that the listed selling price on the summary sheets was manipulated. The homes had been independently valued by appraisers, but different agents were given different listing prices—ranging from 12 percent higher than the actual appraisal to 12 percent lower. Consistent with the power of anchors, the higher the listing price, the higher the agents' valuation and estimated selling price.

Anchors are widely used by people in the persuasion professions, such as advertisers, politicians, real estate agents, and lawyers.

The anchoring effect is most potent when there is a lack of objective information to compare against. Why is a new Patek Philippe watch "worth" $25,000? Because its manufacturer says so? Have you ever gone shopping for a diamond? Did you buy one? How do you know if you got a good deal? Is a wonderful painting by an unknown artist worth $50 or $5,000? Purchases of jewelry and art are particularly vulnerable to anchoring effects because most of us have a great deal of difficulty assessing true value. We are heavily influenced by the initial price set by the seller.

In ambiguous situations, we need to be particularly cautious of trivial factors because they can have a profound effect on anchoring us to an initial position that is hard to deviate from. And implausible anchors can produce large effects.[5] For instance, a television infomercial that promises that you could make $300,000 in the first year of selling a certain product is more likely to motivate you to sign up than one that offered a more realistic $25,000. Because we're unlikely to have any valid reference point to challenge the $300,000 claim, it's easy for shady entrepreneurs to suck in people with outrageous statements.

You can do a couple of things to make yourself less susceptible to anchoring effects. First, be aware of the anchoring bias. Recognize that we're all vulnerable to first impressions, so we have to be vigilant when we receive initial information. You need to particularly scrutinize initial values that seem unusually high or low.[6] Also, you should be cautious when confronted with best- or worst-case scenarios. This is because extreme anchor values produce the largest anchoring effects. "For instance, after considering the probability of a business venture under ideal conditions, it is difficult to arrive at a realistic projection."[7] Finally, use your knowledge of the anchoring effect to improve your negotiation skills. As a buyer, pay little attention to initial offers. Although everyone must have a starting position, these initial offers tend to be extreme and idealistic. Don't let them limit your focus or narrow your options. Conversely, as a seller, you want to do just the opposite. Try to take the initiative by defining an initial price and focus the negotiations around that initial number.

Decision Tips

- Be aware that initial values bias subsequent information.
- Be vigilant to initial values that appear unusually high or low as well as best- and worst-case scenarios.
- As a buyer, pay little attention to initial offers.
- As a seller, try to take the initiative by defining an initial price.

I'll See It When I Believe It: The Selective Perception Bias

It isn't that they can't see the solution.
It's that they can't see the problem.
—G.K. Chesterton

The following represents a classic study in perception. Twenty-three middle-level managers were asked to read a comprehensive case describing the operational activities in a steel company.[1] Six of the 23 executives worked in the area of sales, five in production, four in accounting, and eight in miscellaneous functions. After reading the case, each of these executives was then asked to identify the problem a new company president should deal with first. Eighty-three percent of the sales executives rated sales most important, but only 29 percent of the others did. Similarly, the production executives gave priority to the production area, and the accounting people focused on accounting problems. These findings led to the conclusion that these participants interpreted the cases' priorities in terms of the activities and goals of the functional areas to which the executives were attached. That is, the perception of organizational activities was selectively interpreted by these executives in response to their experience, training, and vested interests.

When situations are ambiguous, as they were in the steel company case, perception tends to be influenced more by an individual's base of interpretation than by the stimulus itself. Attitudes, interests, experiences, and background selectively bias what we see.

The steel case illustrates how departmental affiliation in an organization can bias perceptions, but this bias can be shaped by numerous factors. Age, gender, race, early childhood experiences, occupation, and family status are some other examples. For instance, a 60-year-old is more likely to notice rap music than a 20-year-old because it's less familiar to an older person. Single women often see meaning in off-hand comments made by male suitors that differ considerably from what the men intended. Blacks, Asians, Hispanics, and other minorities, who have experienced a lifetime of discrimination, are much more likely to note and take offense at a racial slur than someone who has never experienced racial discrimination. Couples with children see a world that is very different from that perceived by childless couples. And in relationships, selective perception is often the reason that friends can see problems in our marriages that we can't. Our friends aren't weighted down with the "baggage" of our experiences and expectations.

Do you think the media is fair in covering world events? What's *fair* depends on which side you're on. For instance, a study of pro-Arab and pro-Israeli students found that they both agreed that television news coverage in the United States of an Arab-Israeli conflict during a 10-day period was biased.[2] However, each group of students saw the bias in favor of the other side. On average, pro-Arab students reported that 42 percent of the references to Israel had been favorable and only 26 had been unfavorable. Pro-Israeli students, in contrast, recalled 57 percent of the references to Israel as having been unfavorable and only 16 percent as having been favorable.

The world is far more ambiguous than most of us are willing to admit, and each of us has a unique perceptual base from which we see and interpret this ambiguous world. The result? We're incapable of objectively seeing events around us. Rather, what we do is selectively organize and interpret events based on our biased perceptions and then call this interpretation *reality*. Selective perception biases decision making by influencing the information we pay attention to, the problems we identify, and the alternatives we develop. Because we see a biased world, we can draw unwarranted conclusions from ambiguous situations. This was demonstrated in a study on capital punishment.[3] Proponents and opponents of the death penalty were both asked to read two position papers—one for and the other against capital punishment. Consistent with selective perception, exposure to the conflicting findings only acted to reinforce the views held before reading the position papers. Participants in the study ignored evidence that contradicted their beliefs and actually interpreted the mixed evidence to confirm the validity of their original beliefs.

We can't eliminate selective perception. Each of us brings to every situation the baggage of our past experiences, attitudes, and vested interests. We can, however, actively attempt to minimize our perceptual biases by increasing our awareness, confronting our expectations, and considering how others might interpret the situation.

Begin by acknowledging that both "truth and beauty are in the eye of the beholder." There is no pure objectivity. We all see the world through our unique tainted lenses, which allows us to believe what

> *We're incapable of objectively seeing events around us.*

we want to believe. Next, you need to understand what your perceptual biases are. What expectations do you bring to a situation that might bias the way you see it? Finally, ask yourself whether someone else with different expectations might see the same situation differently. For example, Shawna Clark is 30 years old. She grew up in the 1980s and 1990s—a time of economic optimism. In the spring of 2000, when the stock market began what became a three-year decline, Shawna saw every dip as a "buying opportunity." Every time the Dow would drop 400 or 500 points, she faithfully would put more money into the market. Sadly, by early 2002, she had lost 40 percent of her savings. Shawna's selective-perception problem was created by her experience. She had never seen the stock market maintain sustained losses during her lifetime. All she had ever experienced was a stock market that went up, interrupted by occasional short-term setbacks, so she saw every downturn as an opportunity to buy stocks on the cheap. Her dad, on the other hand, had seen protracted market losses during the 1973-75 recession, and her grandfather had lived through the market declines of the early 1930s. Both her dad and grandfather were less convinced that the market would quickly rebound and did not believe that every decline between 2000 and 2002 was a buying opportunity. Shawna's behavior changed in March 2002, when she challenged herself to see the declining market through the eyes of her dad and grandfather. "I saved myself a lot of grief and money when I looked at market patterns over 70 years instead of just the last 10."

Decision Tips

- Be aware that all our perceptions are biased.
- Assess how your expectations in a situation can bias your perceptions.
- Consider how an impartial outsider might see the situation differently.

I Hear What I Want to Hear: The Confirmation Bias

*Most of our so-called reasoning consists in finding
arguments for going on believing as we already do.*
— J.H. Robinson

Mike Delaney is a fitness nut. Now 42 years old, he has been working out regularly since he was in his late teens. In a typical week, Mike will spend two hours a day, three days a week, lifting weights at his health club. In addition, he runs an average of 50 miles a week. He occasionally breaks up his routine with workouts on a stair climber or putting in an hour on a rowing machine.

In recent months, Mike has been plagued by a number of aches and pains. A lot more than usual. His knees are aching, his Achilles' tendons are sore, and his lower back is bothering him. He called his regular doctor, who recommended he see a sports-medicine specialist. After a thorough exam, the specialist told Mike to cut back on his training. "You're too old to be training this hard. Your body can't take the abuse like it used to. You don't need to work out more than 30 to 45 minutes a day to stay in good health."

Although Mike is annoyed and pained by his injuries, did he follow the doctor's suggestion and cut back on his training? No. Mike says, "If you don't use it, you lose it. I've read where the health benefits of training require intense workouts. My aches and pains are only temporary. I can train through them. If I were to cut back on my training, I'd lose all the work I've done, and my fitness level would just begin to deteriorate."

Mike is suffering from the *confirmation bias*. He is ignoring information he doesn't want to hear and giving greater weight to information that supports his preconceived views.

The rational decision-making process assumes that we objectively gather information. But we don't. As noted in the previous chapter, we *selectively* gather information. The confirmation bias represents a specific case of selective perception. We seek out information that reaffirms our past choices, and we discount information that contradicts past judgments.[1] We also tend to accept information at face value that confirms our preconceived views, while being critical and skeptical of information that challenges these views. Therefore, the information we gather is typically biased toward supporting views we already hold. This confirmation bias influences where we go to collect evidence because we tend to seek out places that are more likely to tell us what we want to hear. It also leads us to give too much weight to supporting information and too little to contradictory information.

Why do we tend to seek out evidence that supports our current beliefs and to dismiss evidence that challenges them? One explanation is consistency.[2] As noted in previous chapters, rational decision making needs to be perceived as consistent. And we can increase our consistency by staying the course and ignoring information that might suggest that our course is wrong. Another explanation is that confirming evidence acts as a reward and is more reinforcing. We tend to be more engaged by things we like than things we don't. Confirming evidence also rewards us by saying we're on the right track, while disconfirming evidence implies we're not as smart as we think we are.[3] A third explanation is that it reduces conflict and complexity. Life and decision making are simpler if we can minimize our exposure to data that challenges the neat, consistent, and uncomplicated world we've created in our heads.[4]

We see the confirmation bias in an array of decisions. For instance, in our dating years, it shapes our relationships when we ignore information that suggests that someone might not be a good match for us. It clouds our career decisions when we stay with a job that limits the use of our talents or when we miss out on new job

> *The confirmation bias influences where we go to collect evidence because we tend to seek out places that are more likely to tell us what we want to hear.*

opportunities because we focus on the pluses of our current job. And it taints our investment decisions when we ignore information that tells us our current investment strategy isn't working.

Unfortunately, the evidence suggests that the confirmation bias is hard to overcome.[5] The obvious solution—to aggressively search out contrary or disconfirming information—has been found to be difficult for people to actually do. Even when individuals have been given extensive instructions stressing the value of disconfirming evidence, it seems to have only modest effects on their judgments. So what can you do? My best advice is to begin by being honest about your motives.[6] Are you seriously trying to get information in order to make an informed decision, or are you just looking for evidence to confirm what you'd like to do? If you're serious about this, then you need to purposely seek out disconfirming information. That means you need to be prepared to hear what you don't want to hear. You'll also need to practice skepticism until it becomes habitual. You have to train yourself to consistently challenge your favored beliefs. In the same way that a defense attorney seeks contradictory evidence to disprove a plaintiff's case, you have to think of reasons why your beliefs might be wrong and then aggressively seek out evidence that might prove them to be so.

Decision Tips

- Become a skeptic.

- Actively look for information that disconfirms your beliefs.

- Consider reasons why your beliefs might be wrong and try to prove them so.

Chapter Eighteen

Is the Glass Half-Empty or Half-Full?
The Framing Bias

First umpire: "Some's balls and some's
strikes and I calls 'em as they is.
Second umpire: "Some's balls and some's
strikes and I calls 'em as I sees 'em."
Third umpire: "Some's balls and some's strikes
but they ain't nothin' till I calls 'em."
—H. Cantril

The following story demonstrates the link between framing and
decision making.[1] Two young priests were heavy smokers and somewhat
troubled about this habit when they were praying. The first asked his
bishop: "Would it be permissible for me to smoke while praying to the
Lord?" The bishop responded with a resounding "No." The second priest
asked the same bishop permission, but worded his question a bit
differently. He asked, "During those moments of weakness when I smoke,
would it be permissible for me to say a prayer to the Lord?" The answer to
the second priest was "Yes, of course, my son." Notice that the way the
two questions were worded changed the decision that the bishop made.

Frames are mental structures we create for interpreting meaning.[2] Because we communicate with language, words shape frames. By changing words, we change the way we see and understand. It often helps to think of framing as analogous to what a photographer does. The visual world is huge and ambiguous. When photographers aim their cameras and focus on a specific shot, they frame their photos. They focus attention on what they believe is most relevant. As decision makers, we do the same thing when we define a problem, review our options, or estimate probabilities. The way we define a problem, for instance, goes a long way toward shaping how it's likely to be solved. As a case in point, a friend of mine has been out of work for nearly a year. He keeps talking about his problem as being "lack of job opportunities." When I listen to him, I hear him saying that he doesn't know what he wants to do, so I see his problem as "lack of goals." My friend spends his days searching for job listings and sending out hundreds of resumes for a wide variety of jobs. Because I've framed his problem as an absence of goals, I'd be spending time assessing my skills and abilities and then trying to refine what it is I'm looking for. Although it's irrelevant which of us is right, the fact is that our actions will differ depending on the frame we choose.

Frames determine which aspects in a situation will be attended to and which will be filtered out. And, like photos, their downside is that they create blind spots. Frames must, by definition, leave things out. So they can distort what we see and create incorrect reference points. By drawing our attention to specific aspects of a situation and highlighting them, while at the same time downplaying or omitting other aspects, frames can lead us astray.

Why might people frame similar problems differently? The answer is that our frames are rooted in our experience, training, and culture.[3] Plastic surgeons look at the same faces you and I do, and they see more imperfect noses. And the training of engineers and artists lead them to see the world differently. Similarly, different cultures teach their young different value frames.[4] The British teach the values of democracy while Cubans are taught the superiority of socialism. Americans value assertiveness; Swedes don't. These values shape what we focus on and what we ignore.

One of the most well-documented findings related to framing is that people treat perceived losses considerably differently than perceived gains.[5] When decision outcomes are framed as avoiding losses, we

> *Plastic surgeons look at the same faces you and I do, and they see more imperfect noses.*

tend to be risk seeking. When framed as a gain, we tend to be risk averse. This difference in risk propensity means the way a potential outcome is described can have a large effect on our behavior. For instance, the way that results from cancer treatment are presented have been shown to influence how people respond.[6] More lung cancer patients select surgery when they're told they have a "68 percent chance of living for more than one year" compared to being told that surgery results in a "32 percent chance of dying by the end of the year." When faced with a decision involving a potential loss, we are more willing to take risks to avoid the loss. This helps explain why so many of us don't sell stocks when we have losses. We focus on how much we'd lose if we sold the stock rather than how much profit we might be giving up if we put that money into another stock. In 2003, a lot of investors continued to believe that high-tech stocks, many of which had dropped more than 80 percent, would rebound: "I paid $90 for Oracle. Now it's $8. It'll come back." We should point out that some high-flying stocks of previous decades—Penn Central, Polaroid, Xerox, Wang, Sunbeam, Smith Corona—never rebounded.

There is no shortage of instances where the way a problem is framed significantly influences the way people respond. In business, for instance, you're more likely to sell an expensive item—a home, art work, or a classic car—if you can successfully frame the sale to a potential buyer as an *investment* rather than an *expense*. And, of course, the politics of gun control in the United States have been largely shaped by the National Rifle Association's (NRA's) argument that gun control is a second amendment "freedom" issue. The NRA has successfully shaped public opinion to think of gun controls as taking away a citizen's right to bear arms.

The recommendations to you are, first, be aware of the frame you're using. What is it emphasizing? What are its weaknesses? Second, make sure your frame appropriately fits the problem. A lot of us get emotionally attached to a certain frame and tend to apply it universally. For instance, although trusting others may be appropriate most of the time, there are times where this frame will lead to a poor decision. Third, try to reframe problems in a different way and see if this changes your decision. For instance, a high school teacher I know, who has taught for several decades, considers all his students lazy and irresponsible. When he began teaching an advanced placement class, this frame got him into trouble. He got a lot better results when he reframed his new class as made up of students who were curious and ambitious. Finally, continually challenge your frame by trying to falsify it. Why might it be wrong? A friend of mine—a social worker—was convinced that work organizations are psychic prisons. She strongly believed that they constrained members by constructing job descriptions, departments, rules, and regulations that limited choice. Her opinion changed somewhat when I challenged her to consider the flaws in this frame. She then proceeded to build a strong case that organizations are cooperative systems, where individuals and groups work together to attain common goals.

Decision Tips

- Be aware of the frame you're using.
- Make sure your frame fits the problem.
- Try to reframe your problem in different ways.
- Challenge your frame by trying to falsify it.

What Have You Done for Me Lately? The Availability Bias

I remember things the way
they should have been.

—T. Capote

In October 2002, the "Beltway Sniper" terrorized the Washington, D.C., area for 23 days, killing 10 people and wounding three others.[1] Four of the people killed were shot in gas stations.

A rational person in the D.C. area would have realized that the likelihood of being shot by the sniper at a gas station, or anywhere else for that matter, was pretty small. However, rationality didn't seem too widespread during the 23-day shooting spree. Thousands of people stayed in their homes, fearful of being shot. Many others decided it was too dangerous to go to gas stations. Statistics, however, suggest that these fears were unfounded. The chances of being killed by a gunshot wound in the United States in any single year is 1 in 25,196. You have a higher probability of dying by accidental poisoning. In fact, your risk of dying in a car accident is far higher than dying by a gunshot wound. On average, in an area the size of D.C. over a 23-day period, about 40 people can be expected to die in traffic accidents. But no one seems particularly alarmed by this statistic.

85

A rational appraisal would tell you that the increased risk of a D.C.-area resident being killed by the sniper during his shooting spree was incredibly small. Other life-threatening risks—such as a car accident—are far more likely, but people don't seem to worry about them.

Were the people who changed their behavior in response to the sniper ignorant of the statistics? Probably not. Rather, they got sucked in by the availability bias.

The *availability bias* says that we tend to remember events that are most available in our memory—those that are the most recent and vivid. This, in turn, distorts our ability to recall events in a balanced manner and results in distorted judgments and probability estimates.[2] One of the most obvious examples of this phenomenon relates to the fear of flying. The objective evidence consistently shows that flying on a commercial airline is one of the safest, if not *the* safest, forms of transportation. For instance, you're far more likely to die in a car than in a plane. The probability of dying in a plane is 1 in 11 million versus 1 in 5,000 for dying in a car crash, yet millions of people don't believe these numbers or have difficulty internalizing them. Why? Because when a plane goes down and people die, it makes headlines. The stories and pictures about these accidents grab at our emotions and become indelibly marked in our memory. Dozens of people die every day in car accidents. However, unless one of those individuals is a friend or relative, or the accident is extraordinary for some reason ("10 People Killed in 50 Car Pile-Up"), these deaths don't affect our behavior or future decisions. The media coverage given to earthquakes, tornadoes, shark attacks, terrorist attacks, and similar dramatic events tends to make them more available in our memory, and, as a result, we tend to think they're more frequent than they are.

The key to understanding this bias is recognizing that you're a product of your experience. What you've seen, read, and experienced shapes your perceptions of risk and probabilities. To the degree that your experiences are biased, your perceptions of risk and probabilities are likely to be inaccurate.

What are the implications of this bias on your decision making? Because most of us don't have balanced experiences, we distort risks and probabilities. We avoid some risks that aren't that risky and ignore risks that we shouldn't ignore. Then we end up making a wide range of poor decisions—for instance, regarding travel, insurance, and exercise. We avoid taking vacations to exotic and interesting places because of unfounded fears that we might be victims of terrorists or kidnappers. Residents of Los Angeles and Seattle run out and buy earthquake insurance right after experiencing a major earthquake when, in actuality, the near-term risk of another major quake has declined. Many people used the highly publicized death of running guru Jim Fixx at age 52 to conclude that exercise was dangerous.

The media coverage given to earthquakes, tornadoes, shark attacks, terrorist attacks, and similar dramatic events tends to make them more available in our memory, and, as a result, we tend to think they're more frequent than they are.

Astute business people have learned how to turn the availability bias to their advantage. Insurance sales people exploit the fact that we're prone to overestimate unlikely events, so they push highly profitable products like earthquake, tornado, fire, and flood insurance. Executives, who understand that "out of sight is out of mind," spend heavily on advertising to keep their products and services vivid in our memory. Film producers understand the power of this bias; that's why they release so many of their best movies near the end of the year. In the quest to win Academy Awards, producers realize that voters are more likely to recall a movie that they saw last month than one they viewed 10 or 11 months ago.

The availability bias is tough to overcome. Nevertheless, I can offer a couple of suggestions. First, don't over-rely on your memory for information prior to making a decision. For major decisions, substitute objective research and data gathering for information drawn from memory. As an example, many bosses recognize that they tend to give greater weight in annual employee reviews to what their employees have done most recently. To help offset that tendency, they keep a journal for each employee of his or her ongoing performance and then update it regularly. They can then refer to this record before making their performance appraisal. A second suggestion is to question your data. Ask yourself this question: Am I being unduly influenced by information that is readily available, recent, or vivid? Finally, a long-term approach would be to expand your experiences. Read more. Travel more. Learn more about diverse peoples and cultures. The wider the breadth of your experiences, the more accurate your perceptions of risk and probabilities are likely to be.

Decision Tips

- Don't over-rely on your memory.

- Ask yourself if you're being unduly influenced by information that is readily available, recent, or vivid.

- Expand your experiences.

Looks Can Be Deceiving:
The Representation Bias

*I don't want to belong to any club
that would have me as a member.*

—G. Marx

A few years ago, a survey found that 66 percent of all African-American boys between the ages of 13 and 18 believed that they could earn a living playing professional sports.[1] In reality, the odds that any high school athlete will play a sport on the professional level are about 10,000 to 1! How could these boys' estimates be so off target?

The answer is that these boys are suffering from the *representation bias*. They are assessing the likelihood of an event based on how closely it resembles some other event or set of events.[2] The media and advertisers bombard young black men with stories of kids who grew up in the African-American community, just like them, and who now earn tens of millions of dollars in the National Basketball Association (NBA), National Football League (NFL), or playing professional baseball. So they begin to believe they, too, can become professional athletes. They are drawing analogies and seeing identical situations where they don't exist.

We can all get taken in by the representation bias at times. For instance, do you ever gamble in a casino? If you've played slot machines, roulette, or blackjack, do you believe in patterns? I do, and I should know better. If a slot machine hasn't paid off for a while, I think it's "due." And I often bet more aggressively when I see that a blackjack dealer is on a "losing streak." Again, I should know better because both these games have random payoffs with the odds always favoring the casino. Chance events are not self-correcting. What has happened in the past has *no* impact on what occurs in the future, yet most of us expect probabilities to average out.[3] The evidence tells us that it's erroneous to believe that the ball on a roulette wheel is more likely to fall on red just because the six previous spins have come up black, but people continue to believe so. Although, in the long run, a fair coin will turn up approximately an equal number of heads and tails, in the short run it's not unusual to get numerous streaks where one side comes up 5, 7, or 10 times in a row.

Millions of people have lost a lot of their investment savings because they didn't understand the representation bias. They put their money in mutual funds, which, in itself, is not a bad decision. Where they got into trouble was in choosing in which mutual fund to invest. Many made the error of choosing a top performer from the previous year. Their logic? Last year's winner is likely to continue to win in the future. Unfortunately for many investors, that logic is flawed. The performance of any single mutual fund tends, over time, to regress toward the mean for all mutual funds. Exceptional levels of performance—whether good or bad—tend to be followed by performances that are more typical for the event. Therefore, last year's top performer is likely to perform closer to the average of all mutual funds this year. And last year's worst performers are likely to improve this year by moving toward the average. For individual stocks, some investment experts recommend using this pattern to beat the market averages.[4] Supporters of the "Dogs of the Dow" investment strategy suggest you buy shares of the ten companies in the 30-stock Dow Jones Industrial Average with the highest dividend yields at the beginning of each year and selling the ones from the year before. The logic here is that the high yields typically reflect a recent drop in the companies' stock prices. Over the years, this strategy has generally worked because it allows you to benefit from the tendency for extremes to regress toward the mean.

Regression toward the mean may be easier to see in sports. When a baseball player, whose season batting average is .220, suddenly goes four for four in a game, do you expect him to do the same in his next game? Probably not. You unconsciously know that, in his next game, he is much more likely to go one for four. Although this may seem obvious to any sports fan, investors don't always see the obvious. As a case in point, tens of millions of people overestimated the growth potential of technology stocks in the late 1990s. They began to believe preposterous "facts" like the NASDAQ market would go up an average of 16 percent a year for the next 10 years. Such a conclusion ignores regression to the mean.

Chance events are not self-correcting. What has happened in the past has no impact on what occurs in the future, yet most of us expect probabilities to average out.

Regression to the mean distorts decisions in two ways.[5] First, people don't expect regression in many situations where it's bound to occur. Second, even when they recognize it, they're often very adept at inventing creative explanations. Hence, we have our beliefs in "streaks" of good and bad luck and explanations like "it's different this time" or "this is a new economy with new rules" in justifying sky-high prices for technology stocks in 1999.

Another illustration of the representation bias relates to sample sizes. For instance, notice the difference between these two statements. "Three out of five analysts surveyed recommend that investors allocate at least 80 percent of their portfolio to stocks" versus "a survey of 2,000 analysts found that 1,200 recommended that at least 80 percent of an investor's portfolio be in stocks." Although, on the surface, these two statements

91

seem alike, they're not. The first statement doesn't tell us whether the "three out of five" means 60 percent or if just means five analysts were surveyed. And if it was 60 percent, how large was the overall sample size? The second statement provides us with a more representative sample in that we know it included 2,000 analysts.

Keep in mind that small sample sizes can provide distorted results. It's equivalent to flipping a fair coin five times and getting five heads. Such a result isn't unusual with small samples. But, if you flipped a coin 1,000 times and it came up heads every time, you'd be safe in saying that it was not a fair coin. The message to you is to be cautious in decisions where you're using information based on small samples. They can bias your judgment.

Based on the evidence, here are suggestions for dealing with the representation bias. First, be careful in drawing comparisons from nonidentical situations. Just because the last person you dated was an artist and that person turned out to be irresponsible and thoughtless doesn't mean that the new person you just met—who also happens to be an artist—will have similar qualities. Second, expect regression toward the mean. Extreme performances—whether positive or negative—tend to be followed by more average performances. Finally, be aware that small sample sizes can distort results. For example, don't rush out to buy a book on the recommendation of four random reviewers and don't choose a building contractor based on positive comments from just two former clients.

Decision Tips

- Be careful in drawing comparisons from nonidentical situations.
- Expect extreme performances to be followed by more average performances.
- Small sample sizes can distort results.

Seeing Patterns That Aren't There: Coping with Randomness

*We must believe in luck. For how else can
we explain the success of those we don't like?*

—E. Satie

The stock market goes up 100 points, and the analysts are quick to tell us that "low inflation and strong consumer confidence" is driving the market up. The next day, the market drops 100 points, and those same analysts tell us the reason is "low inflation is likely to hurt corporate profits and there's increasing fears that the consumer will cut back spending because of heavy debt loads."

Isn't it amazing that these analysts never seem to be lost for an explanation of why the market did what it did? Interestingly, they never seem to show this insight and confidence when it comes to accurately predicting what the market might do tomorrow!

For the uninitiated, it's very easy to begin to believe what these analysts are saying. Let me give you some advice. Ignore these "experts."[1] Their assessment, after the fact, is worthless. It fills time on the financial news networks and space on the business pages of your newspaper, earns some of these analysts millions of dollars a year, and reassures many investors that there is logic and reason behind every movement in the market. But close your eyes and cover your ears. Doing so will probably save you some money.

Human beings have a lot of difficulty dealing with chance. Most of us like to believe we have some control over our world and destiny (see Chapter 6). Although we undoubtedly can control a good part of our future by thoughtful decision making, the truth is that the world will always contain random events. You need to be able to accept this fact, differentiate chance events from those that actually follow established patterns, and avoid trying to create meaning out of random data.

Let's get back to stock price movements. In spite of the fact that short-term stock price changes are essentially random, a large proportion of investors—or their financial advisors—believe they can predict the direction that stock prices will move. For instance, when a group of subjects was given stock prices and trend information, these subjects were approximately 65 percent certain they could predict the direction stocks would change. In actuality, these individuals were correct only 49 percent of the time—about what you'd expect if they were just guessing.[2]

Decision making becomes impaired when we try to create meaning out of random events. Take the purchase of lottery tickets as an example. Have you ever noticed what happens when one ticket outlet sells a big winning ticket and then does it again a short time later? The outlet is bombarded by people wanting to buy tickets there. The thinking is that "Roy's Mini-Mart sold someone a $3 million jackpot ticket in February and sold an $8 million ticket in June. I increase my chances of winning if I buy my lottery tickets at Roy's." Even though the selling of a winning ticket is a chance event, many of us become convinced that a pattern exists—that some outlets are more likely to sell winners--and that we can turn this pattern to our advantage.

Decision making becomes further impaired when we use "fate" to explain random occurrences. Because we have difficulty in believing in chance events, many of us look for logical explanations. When all rational explanations fail us, we seek meaning through terms such as *fate, luck,* and *destiny.*[3] (See the test for Locus on Control in Chapter 6.) Sadly, life-threatening diseases such as multiple sclerosis or breast cancer are random events although we often attribute them to fate, bad luck, or "God's will."

One of the most serious distortions caused by random events is when we turn imaginary patterns into superstitions.[4] These can be completely contrived ("I never make important decisions on a Friday the 13th") or evolve from a certain pattern of behavior that has been reinforced previously ("I always wear my lucky tie to important meetings").

> *In spite of the fact that short-term stock price changes are essentially random, a large proportion of investors believe they can predict the direction that stock prices will move.*

Superstitious rituals, for instance, have been found to be widely practiced by athletes in almost every sport.[5] Although we all engage in some superstitious behavior, it can be debilitating when it affects daily judgments or biases major decisions. At the extreme, some people become controlled by their superstitions—making it nearly impossible for them to change routines or objectively process new information.

Random events happen to everyone, and there is nothing you can do to predict them. (That's why they call them *random*!) So don't try. You have to accept that there are events in life that are outside your control. Ask yourself if patterns can be meaningfully explained or whether they are merely coincidence. Don't attempt to create meaning out of coincidence. Additionally, explicitly confront your superstitions. Identify them and challenge their validity. For every superstition you have, ask yourself these questions. Is this inhibiting me from making changes? Does it create any dysfunctional consequences for me? If you answer "yes" to either of these questions, become a skeptic. Try to identify solid reasons that you should continue to believe in this superstitious behavior. Each time you catch yourself falling back on old habits, force yourself to ignore this superstition.

Decision Tips

- Accept that there are events that are outside your control.

- Don't try to create meaning out of random events.

- Acknowledge your superstitions and challenge their validity.

Chapter Twenty-Two

Gone Is Not Always Forgotten: Understanding Sunk Costs

Consistency requires you to be as ignorant
today as you were a year ago.
—B. Berenson

Nancy Segal, a New York City resident, bought a ticket to the ballet. An hour before she was to leave for the performance, she felt tired and a bit sick. She didn't feel like walking eight blocks to Lincoln Center or sitting for three hours. What she really wanted to do was put her feet up on the couch and spend the evening reading a book, but she forced herself to go to the ballet. Her explanation? "I spent $80 for that ticket, and I wasn't about to waste my money."

Nancy made an irrational decision. She got taken in by the concept of *sunk costs*. If Nancy had been rational, she would have based her decision only on future consequences. So the amount she paid for the ticket shouldn't have affected her future decisions. However, she treated the nonrefundable expenditure as equivalent to a current investment. And it's not. Like Nancy, you'll make more effective decisions if you consider only future benefits and costs rather than those already incurred.[1] Why?

Because the decisions you make today can only influence the future. No current decision can correct the past.

A lot of us get sucked in by sunk costs when making decisions. For instance, do you know anyone who just can't leave food on a plate in a restaurant? I have a friend who, when we eat out, always forces herself to clean her plate even when she's absolutely full. The fact that the food is already paid for—eaten or not—is irrelevant to her. Have you ever had anyone tell you they're unhappy in their relationship? If you asked that person why he or she doesn't move on, the answer is something like "Because I've already put so much time into it." Or have you ever stayed through a movie you hate, rather than walk out, because you paid $8 to see it?

In a classic study, one group of subjects was told to imagine themselves as the head of a firm that manufactured military defense aircraft.[2] The company has already invested $10 million in research to try to build a plane that would not be detected by conventional radar. However, when the project is 90 percent complete, a competitor begins marketing a plane that can go undetected by radar and is much faster and far less costly than the plane your company is developing. As head of the company, subjects were asked if they would invest the last 10 percent of the research funds to finish the project. Then a second group was given the same scenario, but no mention was made of the prior investment. Although 85 percent of the first group said they would complete the project, only 17 percent of the second group said they would spend the additional money. Clearly, the previous expenditure of $10 million influenced the first group's decision whether to continue or to drop this project.

A more recent study of playing time by NBA basketball players found that coaches are influenced by sunk costs.[3] In this instance, sunk costs were defined in terms of selection order in the annual college draft. Although you'd expect rational coaches to play and keep their most productive players, draft order irrationally influenced those decisions. Coaches gave more playing time to their most highly drafted players and retained them longer, even after adjusting for factors such as on-court performance, injuries, and the like.

The common thread through these examples is the consideration of sunk costs. But why do so many of us act irrationally when it comes to ignoring past expenditures of time, money, or effort? Why do we fixate on the past rather than on the future? Because ignoring sunk costs can make us look indecisive, inconsistent, and wasteful.[4] We want to save face and avoid admitting, especially in public, that an earlier decision was a mistake. "I've got too much invested to quit now" is a phrase many of us have used too often. We also want to appear consistent. This is because consistency is a key element of rationality. Because most advanced societies value consistency and persistence, we want to look good to others, and we can do this by "staying the course." Finally, many of us desire to avoid appearing wasteful because, in most circles, wastefulness is seen as an undesirable trait.

So how can a knowledge of sunk costs help you to make better decisions? First, the decisions you make today influence only the future, not the past. So don't pay attention to past losses and costs when making decisions.[5] That is, ignore sunk costs. In terms of continuing a relationship, for instance, ask yourself, "If I were going out on a date with this person for the first time today, would I want to see them again?"

> *The decisions you make today influence only the future, not the past. So don't pay attention to past losses and costs when making decisions.*

Second, it's OK to admit mistakes. If you have trouble conceding errors, ask yourself this: Why does admitting to an earlier mistake distress me? The idea here is to know when to say stop. You want to be able to distinguish those situations where persistence in pursuing a previously set course will pay off and when it's just misdirected.

Third, consistency isn't always a desirable trait. Flexibility can also be an asset. It's all right to be inconsistent if you can objectively justify it. A past decision, made under a certain set of conditions, may no longer be appropriate if those conditions have changed.[6] Your previous decision wasn't necessarily wrong; it just no longer fits the prior conditions it was made under.

Decision Tips

- Ignore sunk costs.
- It's OK to admit mistakes.
- You don't always have to be consistent.

Chapter Twenty-Three

Keep It Simple:
The Limited Search Error

Everything should be made as simple
as possible, but not simpler.

—A. Einstein

Todd Lucci graduated from the University of Illinois in 1993. Although he majored in psychology and talked about going to graduate school and eventually pursuing a career as a therapist, his dad encouraged him to return to his hometown of Chicago and work in the family's restaurant business. Todd's dad and uncle own and operate six McDonald's franchises in northern Illinois.

Upon graduation, Todd packed up and returned to Chicago. He joined the family business, bought a home, married, and now has two small children. Todd recently reflected on that decision he made 10 years ago:

> I guess it was almost a non-decision. My dad said come into the business and it just seemed like the easy thing to do. I knew what I'd be getting into. I had worked for dad on weekends and summers since I was 15. I chose the known rather than the unknown.

Now, as I look back, I think of what could have been. I could have gone back to grad school. I'm sure I could have gotten scholarships and loans to cover the cost. I could have gotten a degree in counseling psychology and become a therapist. I know I would have been good at it. I often think how much more fulfilling my life might have been if I hadn't been so quick to just accept my dad's offer. But that was the easy thing to do. I really didn't consider my other options.

Todd's decision to join his family's business after graduating from college was a major life-changing event. Unfortunately for Todd, he didn't give it the time and thought that he should have. He made no effort to follow the rational decision-making process we described in Chapter 2. He chose, instead, to limit his search.

When faced with a complex problem, we construct a simplified model that extracts the essential features from the problem without capturing all its intricacies.

When faced with complex decisions, the evidence indicates that we are all prone to try to simplify the process by limiting our search efforts.[1] Most of us respond to complexity by reducing a problem to a level at which it can be readily understood. We do this because it's impossible for us to assimilate and understand all the information needed to optimize the decision. We don't have the time, knowledge, and other resources assumed in the rational decision-making process. So, as briefly described in Chapter 3, we satisfice.

The process we use has been described as *bounded rationality*. When faced with a complex problem, we construct a simplified model that extracts the essential features from the problem without capturing all its intricacies.[2]

How does bounded rationality work for the typical individual? After a problem is identified, the search for criteria and alternatives begins, but the list of criteria is likely to be far from exhaustive. The decision maker will identify a limited list made up of the more obvious choices. These are the choices that are easy to find and that tend to be highly visible. In most cases, the choices will represent familiar criteria and tried-and-true solutions. After a limited set of alternatives is identified, the decision maker will begin reviewing them. However, the review will not be comprehensive. Not all the alternatives will be evaluated carefully. Instead, the decision maker will begin with alternatives that differ only in a relatively small degree from the choice currently in effect. Following along familiar and well-worn paths, the decision maker will proceed to review alternatives only until he or she identifies an alternative that is "good enough"—one that meets an acceptable level of performance. The first alternative that meets the "good enough" criterion ends the search. So the final solution represents a satisficing choice rather than an optimum one.

One of the more interesting features of bounded rationality is that the order in which alternatives are considered becomes critical. In the fully rational decision process, all alternatives are eventually listed in order of preference. Because all alternatives are considered, the initial order in which they are evaluated is irrelevant. That is, every potential solution gets a full and complete evaluation. But this isn't the case with bounded rationality. If a problem has more than one potential solution, the satisficing choice will be the first acceptable one the decision maker encounters. And because decision makers are using a simple and limited search procedure, they typically begin by identifying alternatives that are obvious, ones with which they are familiar, and those not too far from the status quo. Those solutions that depart least from the status quo and meet the decision criteria are most likely to be selected. So a unique and creative alternative may present an optimizing solution to the problem, but it's unlikely to be chosen because an acceptable solution will be identified well before the decision maker is required to search very far beyond the status quo.

Following bounded rationality, we can make several predictions. We simplify complex decisions by reducing the number of criteria and options, and we terminate the process as soon as we identify an alternative that is good enough. In addition, we aren't likely to develop alternatives that are much different than the status quo because we look at alternatives sequentially, begin with those that are least different, and usually find a satisficing choice before we have to come up with truly innovative options.

Another insight related to limited search is that, early in the decision process, many of us pare down the number of alternatives we're willing to consider.[3] Rather than develop an exhaustive list of alternatives and devote energy into assessing each, we early on reduce the set of viable alternatives to a manageable number—often just one or two. We do this by asking ourselves whether an alternative will meet one of three tests: Is it compatible with my basic principles or values? Is it compatible with my goals? Is it compatible with my plans for achieving those goals? If an alternative doesn't pass these three tests, we screen it out. This line of research is consistent with satisficing and confirms that decision making is rarely as comprehensive as the rational process would suggest. Additionally, it tells us that the limiting process is severe—often reducing the number of viable alternatives to one or two; that this paring is done early in the decision process rather than later; and that we apply three tests of compatibility with our values, goals, and plans—to arrive at our reduced set.

We're all susceptible to the limited-search error. That doesn't mean, however, that we can't overtly take steps to try to reduce it. That effort can begin by keeping an open mind. Don't judge alternatives prematurely. Be aware of our tendency, especially with complex problems, to simplify them and speed up the search for a solution. Take the time to increase your options. Even if an obvious alternative looks perfect, resist your tendency to choose it quickly and conclude the process. Keep searching to expand your set of alternatives. Finally, be creative in your search for alternatives. In addition to the obvious, look "outside the box" to consider strange, unconventional, and previously untried options. The more alternatives you can generate, and the more diverse those alternatives, the greater your chance of finding an outstanding one.

Decision Tips

- Don't judge alternatives prematurely.

- Increase your options.

- Look "outside the box" for nonobvious alternatives.

Chapter Twenty-Four

Losing Your Head in the Heat of Battle: The Emotional Involvement Error

Ninety percent of our lives
is governed by emotion.
—*A. N. Whitehead*

The odometer on Ray Davis' Toyota Camry turned 120,000 miles last week. Ray knew he was due for a new car. He figured it was now only a matter of time before he was overwhelmed with maintenance costs—something he definitely wanted to avoid.

This time around, Ray was going to treat himself to something sexier than his Camry. He wanted a new Volvo C70. A red convertible. He'd seen one at a car show, and it was love at first sight. So two nights ago, Ray went on the Internet and did some research. He read reviews on the car. He checked out J.D. Powers for its quality ratings, and he liked what he read about the C70. He also found a Web site that gave retail prices, dealer invoice costs, and what he should expect to pay. Armed with his pricing information, he went to his local Volvo dealer last night. On arrival, he saw the dealer had four C70 convertibles in stock—two white, one black, and one red. Each had the same retail sticker price on the windshield—$47,275.

Ray calculated that his dealer paid $44,425 for each of the convertibles, and, from his research, he figured he should be able to buy a car at $700 over dealer's cost or about $2,100 under list. After more than an hour of negotiations, Ray drove out in his new red convertible. But he paid $47,050. He was only able to bargain $225 off the sticker price.

This morning, a calmer and cooler Ray Davis realized that he had paid too much for his car because he'd allowed his emotions to cloud his judgment. He wanted that red convertible and his enthusiasm was evident as soon as he walked into the Volvo showroom. Meanwhile, the car salesman played on Ray's emotions—talking up the joy of a convertible, the fun of driving a red car, and the beauty of the optional chrome wheels. After a test drive, Ray was putty in the salesman's hands. In retrospect, Ray now realizes he probably paid almost $2,000 more than he should have because he allowed his emotions to get the best of him.

Emotions can have a powerful effect on decisions. They can influence both the process by which a decision is made and, as in Ray Davis' case, the decision's final outcome. We're all human, and we all have emotions. As you'll see in this chapter, the challenge we face is to manage our emotions so they do a minimal amount of damage.

Emotions that most of us have experienced at one time or another include happiness, surprise, hope, fear, anxiety, sadness, despair, anger, and disgust.[1] And everyone, at times, gets emotional. Some people, however, allow their emotions to overwhelm their decisions, especially when they're overly excited or under stress. Take a second and look back at your test score for Chapter 9. Remember, low scores indicate you have trouble controlling your emotions. The lower your score, the more you need to aggressively try to control the negative aspects of emotions.

The rational decision process is assumed to be emotion free, and many of the decisions we have to make can be made by keeping our feelings on hold. But a lot can't. For instance, you wouldn't want romantic decisions—falling in love, choosing to marry, or buying a special gift for a loved one—to be made without emotion. And

Negative emotions tend to narrow our attention, speed up the decision process, and lead to impulsive actions.

sometimes decisions that you later recognize turned out very well—quitting a frustrating job in the heat of an argument, buying a piece of art that you "fell in love with", or tearing up your credit cards out of frustration with increasing debt—are largely driven by emotions. But we're concerned with situations where emotions significantly undermine rationality and lead to unhappy outcomes. Negative emotions tend to narrow our attention, speed up the decision process, and lead to impulsive actions. This, in turn, often results in postdecision regret.[2] Most of us have experienced situations where we got caught up in the heat of the moment, made a rash decision, and later regretted it.

The evidence indicates that rationality is most likely to be undermined when we allow emotions to direct us away from our long-term goals, when we have to make hard choices under stress, and when we're overly excited.[3]

Negative emotions—such as anger, frustration, hate, and revenge—tend to surface when we're faced with the need to make difficult and stressful choices between important goals. For instance, conflicts between career and family, maintaining the good life and living within your budget, or respecting the law when we see legal abuses can be a source of negative emotions. When a drunk driver kills an innocent child and then walks away with no jail time, it can take great emotional control by the child's parents to refrain from taking revenge.

In recent years, many investors have allowed their emotional impulses to override their rational thinking.[4] They bought overpriced stocks in the late-1990s in the heat of "irrational exuberance." Then, when the market went into decline, they sold everything out of fear and frustration. Although none of us can accurately predict the stock market's future, one thing is certain. Making critical investment decisions with your retirement nest egg should not be based on impulsive mood swings.

The first step toward managing emotions is to recognize that they can influence your decisions. Whether that influence is positive or negative depends on the type of the decision, its importance, your level of arousal, and your level of awareness. If you scored low on the test in Chapter 9, you need to be particularly vigilant so as not to let your emotions control your choices. Second, delay making major decisions when you're stressed out or excited. Most decisions can be delayed for a day or two with minimal consequences. Third, if you can't delay the decision, use others as a sounding board. Review your decision with friends or relatives who aren't emotionally involved. Fourth, take the time to expand your options. You're less likely to make an impulsive choice if you have to assess and weigh additional alternatives. Finally, keep focused on your long-term goals. If you must make a decision and emotions are involved, you're less likely to take an impulsive action that you'll later regret if you make sure it fits with your long-term plans.

Decision Tips

- Recognize that emotions can influence decisions.
- Delay making major decisions when you're stressed out or excited.
- Use others, who aren't emotionally involved, as a sounding board.
- Expand your options.
- Focus on long-term goals.

Chapter Twenty-Five

Who You Gonna Blame?
The Self-Serving Bias

The man who can smile when things go wrong
has thought of someone he can blame it on.

—*Anonymous*

In May 1999, Maria Walker's husband died of a brain tumor. He left her with a home that was paid for and about $350,000. Only 33 years old at the time, Maria knew she would need this money to sustain her lifestyle in the years to come. And uncertain how to invest, she turned the money over to a long-time friend of her late husband, Brion Randall, who was a broker with Merrill Lynch.[1] As a friend, Maria trusted Brion to invest her money well.

First, Brion invested Maria's inheritance in blue chip stocks like Wal-Mart and IBM. However, as the price of high-tech stocks skyrocketed in late 1999, he advised Maria to dump the conservative stocks and become more aggressive. She gave him the go-ahead. By August 2000, Maria's account was made up entirely of tech stocks. And the value of Maria's portfolio grew. In less than a year, her initial $350,000 investment had grown to more than $500,000. Maria, meanwhile, was enjoying the benefits of her increased wealth. Her Visa bill alone was now averaging more than $4,000 a month. "You rock!" she repeatedly told Mr. Randall.

You can probably imagine where this story is going. Brion Randall continued to tout the profit potential in tech stocks, while the value of those stocks fell. By January 2002, the value of Maria's portfolio had dropped to less than $76,000.

Maria was crushed. She had believed in Mr. Randall. Now she had to face the hard reality that much of her inheritance was gone. And while Maria was applauding her smarts in deciding to turn her money over to Mr. Randall when her investments were increasing in value, now he was a *persona non grata*. She held him personally responsible for her losses. Mr. Randall, on the other hand, refused to accept blame for Maria's shrunken portfolio. He blamed poor advice from Merrill Lynch analysts and Maria's own greed.

Maria's investment experience is not unique. During the high-tech stock market rally between 1996 and 2000, investors were quick to brag about their expertise and take credit for their investing smarts. However, when the market imploded and eventually declined more than 75 percent, most of those same investors looked for someone to blame—their brokers, the investment analysts who kept hyping technology stocks, executives who fudged their company's books, and even the Federal Reserve for not cutting interest rates fast enough.

This stock market example illustrates a well-known human tendency. It's called *the self-serving bias*.[2] We are quick to take credit for our successes and to blame failures on outside factors.

There is an extensive amount of evidence to support that we attribute our successes to internal factors such as ability or effort, while putting the blame for our failures on external factors such as bad luck or chance. However, we're not so kind when judging others. When looking at others' decisions, we tend to *underestimate* the influence of external factors or outside causes and *overestimate* the influence of internal or personal factors. So when I lose money in the stock market, I've experienced bad luck or gotten bad advice. When *you* lose money in the market, I think you made a bad decision!

Attributions can help us to better understand how we and others explain our decisions. They tell us we should be alert to our own tendency to hold others fully accountable for their shortcomings, while being far more tolerant of our own. For instance, millions of people suffer from alcohol dependency. When a group of alcoholics were asked to explain their own and "others"

> *When I lose money in the stock market, I've experienced bad luck or gotten bad advice. When* you *lose money in the market, I think you made a bad decision!*

relapses, they came up with very different explanations.[3] The relapses of others were attributed to internal causes—like lack of discipline or willpower. The alcoholics' own relapses, however, were more likely to be blamed on outside forces such as peer pressure from alcohol-dependent friends.

We don't assess the outcomes of our decisions objectively. Our willingness to accept responsibility for our decisions depends on whether the outcome was positive or negative and whether we're judging ourselves or others. So be alert to the fact that, when you screw up, you tend to want to place the blame elsewhere. When you succeed, you want to accept credit. Both of these responses can you get you into trouble. No matter how skilled you are at decision making, no one bats a thousand. There are factors outside our control that can lead to unplanned negative outcomes. And we need to be careful in taking too much credit for our successes.

Moreover, because we're not very good at assessing the cause of our decision outcomes, we often learn the wrong lessons from previous experiences. We become overly confident when we have a string of successes—thinking we have greater control over outcomes than we really do. We also may be unwilling to accept responsibility for decisions we've made that didn't turn out as we had planned.

How can we manage the self-serving bias? First, we need to be aware of this tendency. Be careful about being too confident in extrapolating from past successes to future successes or in placing blame for your setbacks. You're probably not as smart or as unlucky as you think you are. Second, practice challenging your natural inclinations. For instance, when things go well, ask yourself this: What *fortuitous factors* might have helped this happen? When things go bad, ask yourself: What did *I do* that may have precipitated this?

Decision Tips

- Be aware of the self-serving bias.
- Challenge your natural inclinations to make incorrect attributions.

Chapter Twenty-Six

I Knew It All The Time:
The Hindsight Bias

Hindsight is an exact science.

—G. Bellamy

D arren and Jenny were on their first trip to France. After spending a week in Paris, they rented a car and began a five-day tour of the Loire Valley. Darren agreed to drive as long as Jenny would do the navigating. Armed with several maps and her English-French dictionary, Jenny began plotting their route. However, not more than an hour out of Paris, the couple was having trouble finding the road that would take them to their first stop in Montrichard. They pulled over to a rest stop, and together they studied the maps. Nothing made much sense. Jenny thought they should take N20. Darren wasn't convinced. "The maps sure aren't clear," said Darren. "I don't know. Maybe we'd be better off to take the road marked N152." Jenny continued to argue for N20. Darren acquiesced, and they followed Jenny's suggestion. An hour and a half later, they finally made it to Montrichard. As they were checking in to their hotel, Darren told the hotel concierge how they had gotten lost and how difficult it was to follow N20. The concierge then explained that they would have made the trip in half the time if they had taken Route N152. Turning to Jenny, Darren exclaimed, "I knew it! I told you that N152 was the right road to take, but you wouldn't listen to me." Jenny shook her head and quietly muttered, "Yeah, Darren, *now* you're sure, but you weren't so sure a few hours ago!"

Darren has just demonstrated the *hindsight bias*. This is the tendency for us to believe falsely that we'd have accurately predicted the outcome of an event, after that outcome is actually known.[1] When something happens and we have accurate feedback on the outcome, we seem to be pretty good at concluding that this outcome was relatively obvious. This applies to a wide range of activities. For instance, a lot more people seem to have been sure about the inevitability of who would win the Super Bowl on the day *after* the game than they were the day *before*.[2]

> *When something happens and we have accurate feedback on the outcome, we seem to be pretty good at concluding that this outcome was relatively obvious.*

What explains the hindsight bias? We apparently aren't very good at recalling the way an uncertain event appeared to us *before* we find out the actual results of that event. On the other hand, we seem to be fairly well adept at reconstructing the past by overestimating what we knew beforehand based upon what we learned later. So the hindsight bias seems to be a result of both selective memory and our ability to reconstruct earlier predictions.[3]

An example of how the hindsight bias works is illustrated in an experiment with college students during the impeachment trial of President Clinton.[4] Thirty-four students were asked to estimate the chance that Clinton would be convicted or acquitted at four points in time: (1) 22 days before the verdict, (2) 3 days before the verdict, (3) 4 days after the verdict, and (4) 11 days after the verdict. Comparison of individual responses during these four periods revealed that the students' estimates changed over time. Four days after the verdict, the students correctly recalled that their estimates of the likelihood of conviction had shifted toward greater accuracy over time. However, a week later, they incorrectly believed that they had been far more certain all along that Clinton wouldn't be convicted. In other words, the students reinvented their earlier estimates to more accurately match the eventual outcome.

The hindsight bias reduces our ability to learn from the past. It permits us to think that we're better at making predictions than we really are and can result in our being more confident about the accuracy of future decisions than we have a right to be. If, for instance, your actual predictive accuracy is only 40 percent, but you think it's 90 percent, you're likely to become falsely overconfident and less vigilant in questioning your predictive skills.

As noted in a number of previous chapters, awareness alone is often enough to significantly reduce an error or bias. Unfortunately, this doesn't seem to be the case with hindsight.[5] The forces of our selective memory and our ability to reinvent the past are just too powerful. So is there anything you can do? Yes. The most effective way to lessen the hindsight bias is to make yourself consider alternative reasons why the results from a given event might have turned out differently.[6] So, for instance, if you had expected President Clinton to be acquitted, try considering why he might have been convicted. By continually challenging yourself to look at alternative outcomes, you reduce the hindsight bias. Remember, if you only look at the reasons why an event turned out as it did, you tend to overestimate how inevitable that outcome was, and you significantly undermine opportunities to learn from your mistakes.

Decision Tips

- Awareness alone of the hindsight bias isn't enough to lessen the bias' impact.
- Make yourself consider alternative reasons why results might have turned out differently.

Part Four

Advice Your Mother Never Gave You

Chapter
Twenty-Seven

Clear Goals and Preferences Make Choosing a Lot Easier

If you don't know where you're going,
every road will get you nowhere.
—H. Kissinger

D ee Moore was proud of her newfound decision-making skills and so was her husband. Dee no longer drove everyone around her nuts when she went into a restaurant, spending 15 minutes or more trying to make up her mind what she was going to eat. Dee attributes her new ability for making faster decisions to focusing on goals. "I know it sounds silly," Dee commented, "but I realized my problem was that I went into restaurants with no preconceived idea of what I wanted to eat. So I felt I had to carefully scrutinize everything on the menu." The new, goal-oriented Dee described her revised approach to restaurant ordering. "Now when I go into a place, I try to come up with general ideas of what I'd like to eat and what I wouldn't beforehand. So I might say 'I don't want beef or chicken but I want something spicy' or 'I want something light, with a lot of greens.' This approach allows me to quickly eliminate a good portion of items on most menus."

Dee has come to recognize what career and financial advisors have been preaching for decades—you gotta have goals! Without clear and consistent goals, you will continually have trouble making rational decisions in a timely manner. Moreover, when you see people who seem to make inconsistent decisions or who dwell for what seems like an eternity before being able to make up their mind, more often than not the problem can be traced to an absence of clear goals. Regardless of whether we're looking at a mundane decision like ordering in a restaurant or a major decision, such as choosing a career, failure to have clear goals will almost always lead to disappointing outcomes.

Rationality implies consistency, and clear goals are necessary to be consistent. A friend of mine has had half a dozen different jobs in the past 10 years. He's sold cellular phones in a retail store, conducted training seminars, been a substitute teacher in a high school, and repaired cameras. He's 46 years old and has a college degree in English and a masters degree in fine arts, yet he's clearly lost. He tells me he doesn't know what he wants to do. He's not even sure what he's good at. Because he has no clear goals, he wastes a lot of time actively pursuing every job he hears about—even when he's barely qualified. Meanwhile, his erratic career path has begun to turn off prospective employers. In a society that values goals and consistency, my friend's lack of a clear career path is rapidly beginning to cut off job opportunities.

The failure to plan ahead has been described as the single greatest impediment to efficient decision making.[1] Most people seem to have difficulty looking beyond the very near term. This tendency may be most evident when it comes to financial decisions. As we noted in Chapter 14, people find it easy to run up large credit card balances because they can't see the long-term implications from their need to satisfy immediate desires. Many people also find it impossible to save toward retirement. The result is that we have a huge segment of the population that has acquired a "lottery mentality." They have pinned their future on winning the lottery, making a killing in the stock market, inheriting a fortune, winning a huge legal settlement, or the like.

We all have a bias toward the known. When assessing options, we tend to give more weight and substance to that which is more concrete and vivid at the expense of options that are intangible and ambiguous.[2] Hence the power of the immediate donut versus the

The failure to plan ahead has been described as the single greatest impediment to efficient decision making.

long-term satisfaction of losing weight. This bias underscores why we need goals. Without them, we tend to be shortsighted, focusing on options that provide relatively certain outcomes and undervaluing long-run consequences.

Why do we have so much trouble creating and staying with goals? The answer is conflict. Conflict isn't relevant in the purely rational decision process. It's merely assumed that we will select the alternative that provides the highest value. But in the real world, it's often difficult to make decisions because of conflicts. What provides the highest value isn't necessarily obvious. For instance, how do we trade off costs against benefits, risk against value, or immediate satisfaction against future discomfort?[3] If one alternative is clearly superior in all essential respects to others, there is no conflict, and the decision choice is easy. But that's rarely the case. For instance, no potential spouse will be perfect. You consider personality, intelligence, physical appearance, interests, values, finances, and other relevant criteria in the people you date. Then you decide which criteria are more important than others, and you make trade-offs. The key point here is that the clearer your goals, the easier it is to resolve conflicts and make trade-offs. As with my friend who had difficulty making career choices, if you don't have goals and priorities in looking for a spouse, every option looks viable.

If you don't know what you want to accomplish, it's difficult—if not impossible—to make rational decisions. So you need to know your goals and preferences. You can start by assessing your values and priorities. What's important to you? Avoid being influenced by societal pressures and social norms. Try to get inside yourself to see what makes *you* happy. For instance, just because everyone you know says that success means owning a big home on a couple of acres doesn't mean that's your definition of success. You might be happiest in a downtown condo that allows you the convenience of urban living and worry-free travel. After you know your values and priorities, you can derive your goals. Where do you want to be in a year? 10 years? 30 years? The clearer and more specific you can be in defining your goals, the easier it will be for you to assess whether the decisions you're making are leading you toward those goals. And the easier it will be to eliminate options that will lead you away from those goals. Finally, regularly test your alternatives against your goals for consistency. You want to stay on track. To do so, you need to check whether your decisions are consistently moving you closer to your goals.

Decision Tips

- Know your values and priorities.

- Know your goals.

- Test alternatives against your goals for consistency.

Choosing Not to Decide
Is Still a Decision

*No problem is so big and complicated
that it can't be run away from.*
—C. Schulz

"Where did the years go?" asked Cindy Tang. "It seems just like yesterday that I got out of school and joined The Eye Care Center as an optometrist. The years went by and colleagues came and went. I occasionally thought about looking at other places to work, but I never acted on it. So here I am—having worked for the same employer in the same location for my entire career."

"I just came back from my 25th college reunion. Sue, my roommate during my senior year, had changed careers three times and lived in five or six different cities. A couple of my sorority sisters had had a dozen different jobs and had moved up the corporate ladder. The whole experience made me wonder. Did I do something wrong? Did I miss opportunities? Was I afraid of change?"

Cindy Tang is guilty of an error of omission. She never realized that the decision process isn't limited to active choices that involve change. Doing nothing is a decision! It's a decision to maintain the status quo. And in the case of Cindy Tang, her decision to *not* look for other jobs or *not* pursue advancement possibilities shaped her career every bit as much as her friends' active decisions shaped theirs.

> *Doing nothing is a decision! It's a decision to maintain the status quo.*

You can maintain the status quo by following either of two paths—one active and the other passive. You can rationally assess your current situation, identify your options, carefully review the strengths and weaknesses of these options, and conclude that no new alternative is superior to the path you're currently taking. This active approach is fully consistent with rational decision making. Our concern here, however, is with the passive approach—where the current path is followed only because you've failed to consider your other options.

Inexperienced decision makers can get caught in an inaction trap.[1] There are several explanations on why this might happen. One is fear of change. For many people, no matter how bad the status quo is, at least it's a known. Change imposes an unknown ingredient that can be frightening to many. A second possible explanation is satisfaction with the status quo. Many decision makers are inactive because they have no motivation to change. Third is just laziness. Doing nothing is the path of least resistance. Such individuals are often disorganized and have difficulty in doing the "legwork" necessary for making a rational choice. A fourth explanation is unawareness. People do nothing because they never overtly think about pursuing a different path.

History is replete with decision blunders that can be traced to passive inaction. In the 1930s, for instance, the United States watched as Germany built its war capabilities. By the time the United States decided to take action, the forces leading to World War II were already in place. In the 1980s, major retailers like Sears and Kmart paid no attention and took no action in response to the rapid expansion pursued by Wal-Mart. By the time they decided to do something, it was too late. Wal-Mart had stolen much of their customer base.

What applies to countries and companies also applies to individuals. We continue pursuing a course of action even though, by taking an active decision stance, we could probably change things for the better. We continue to smoke because we never directly confront stopping. We never buy life insurance because we never carefully consider the benefits it might provide. We never get a health checkup—not because we purposely avoid going to the doctor—but rather because we never think of "getting a physical" as a decision.

How do you counter the nondecision decision? The first step is awareness. You can't opt out of decisions by ignoring them. To do so is merely making a decision to continue along the path you're on. That path may be the one you want, but the astute decision maker recognizes that there are costs associated with maintaining the status quo as well as with change. You also need to directly challenge the status quo. It's not merely enough to know that doing nothing is a decision. You also need to occasionally justify why you *shouldn't* pursue another path from the one you're currently on. Are you happy in your current job? Is your relationship fulfilling? Do you have habits that make your life less satisfying? You can't improve your life if you don't confront whether the choices you made in the past would be the same ones you'd make today. To determine this, you have to make an active decision. Remember, in the rational decision process (see Chapter 2), the first step is to identify and define the problem. So you may need to create a problem or question if there might be a problem, if one isn't obvious. Interestingly, studies demonstrate that although, in the short term, people may experience regret for actions taken, in the long run, inactions are regretted more.[2] Finally, consider the costs of inaction. Too often we focus only on the risks associated with change. You're less likely to get caught up in decision inaction if you also address the risks from doing nothing.

Decision Tips

- The decision to do nothing is a decision to maintain the status quo.

- Regularly question why you shouldn't pursue another path from your current one.

- Consider the costs from doing nothing.

Chapter
Twenty-Nine

Decisions Are Not Made in Isolation

No amount of sophistication is going to ally the fact
that all your knowledge is about the past and all
your decisions are about the future.
—I.E. Wilson

Two years ago, Julie bought a puppy. She'd been talking about getting a dog for a long time, and she finally decided to get one. "Garth," a golden retriever, now weighs nearly 100 pounds and provides Julie with a wealth of love and companionship. But, as Julie has learned, having a dog has its down sides. She had to spend $1,200 to fence in her small backyard. Because Garth loves to romp and play, Julie has to take him on regular visits to the park. Julie also has to find time to take Garth for grooming every few months and for his occasional visits to the vet when he's not feeling too well. In addition, Julie's active travel schedule now has to be coordinated with hiring a dog sitter or taking Garth to a kennel.

Julie's experience illustrates that decisions are not made in isolation. Buying Garth set in motion a number of future decisions and imposed constraints on some of those decisions. Almost every decision you make is constrained by those decisions that preceded it and limits the decisions you'll make in the future. That is, decisions in the real world are linked and interconnected.

The rational decision process described in Chapter 2 is simplistic and fails to capture this linkage. The rational process is discrete and closed. It assumes that every decision is an isolated event, with a clear beginning and a clear ending. But that's not the way it is in reality. Julie's travel decisions today, for instance, are influenced by the decision she made two years ago to buy a dog. Still, many of us fail to grasp this connectivity between our choices. We make a decision as if it has no bearing on future decisions, and that's a mistake. The options you have available today are a result of choices you made in the past.

It can be helpful to think of single decisions as points in a stream of decisions. Every decision comes with a history and baggage from decisions that preceded it. It doesn't exist in a vacuum. It has a context. And every current decision will limit future decisions.

There is no shortage of examples to illustrate that every decision is actually part of a stream of decisions. For instance, in the political arena, U.S. President George W. Bush's economic and foreign policies are largely limited by the choices made by Bill Clinton, Bush's father, Jimmy Carter, Ronald Reagan, and decades of previous presidential decisions. Issues in the Arab-Israeli conflict that current negotiators have to deal with go back to decisions made in the 1940s and earlier.

Julie's decision to get a dog set in motion a number of additional decisions and limited still others. In a similar vein, major decisions can create overwhelming constraints on later decisions and dramatically change your life. A friend of mine moved from Ann Arbor, Michigan, to Washington, D.C. Ever since, she continually complains about the difficulty of meeting men. Her decision to move to D.C., where the female/male ratio is nearly 3-to-1, is clearly limiting her current social life. The decision to smoke cigarettes, not attend college, select your first full-time job, choose a spouse, have a child, or buy a home are all major decisions that will limit your future choices.

Rationality demands that you think through your decisions before you act. But my argument here goes further. To maintain rationality for the long term, you need to consider decisions in context. Decisions made in the past are ghosts that continually haunt current choices, so what you decide today will influence

Almost every decision you make is constrained by those decisions that preceded it and limits the decisions you'll make in the future.

and constrain your choices tomorrow. A decision that, at a moment in time, may seem inconsequential, can haunt you for years into the future. For instance, your choice of a college major may seem trivial, but it's likely to shape the type of job you'll get, which will determine where you might live, how much you'll make, and even the type of friends you'll have. Similarly, although no one is likely to argue that choosing a spouse is a minor decision, a woman friend understood the full ramifications of this decision when she once remarked to me that "who a woman marries will determine where she lives, the size of her home, where she shops, who many of her friends are, how she spends her evenings, where she goes on her vacations, or where her kids will go to college, and probably even where she'll be buried."

In addition to looking at decisions in context, you can improve your decision making by looking ahead and ensuring that current decisions fit with your goals. Look ahead to see the future consequences of today's action. By doing so, you'll lessen the chance that you'll ignore or limit future opportunities. Because today's decisions will shape and constrain future decisions, you need to assess where today's decisions fit into your future. You want to make sure the commitments you're making today are consistent with your goals a month from now, a year from now, 10 years down the road, and so forth.

Decision Tips

- Consider decisions in context.

- Look ahead to the future consequences of today's action.

- Link current decisions to future goals.

All Decisions Aren't Important

*As you go through life, there are thousands of little
forks in the road, and there are a few really big forks
—those moments of reckoning, moments of truth.*

—L. Iacocca

Mike was overwhelmed. He wanted a large-screen television bad.
Most of his friends had one. Now it was his turn to move up. Based on his
experience watching sporting events at his buddys' apartments, Mike was
sure he wanted at least a 36-inch screen.

Mike spent a Saturday afternoon going from Best Buy to Circuit City to
the Electronic Emporium. He saw TVs that ranged in size from 36 inches
to 60 inches. He saw flat screens, plasmas, front projectors, and back
projectors. He looked at sets made by Sony, Panasonic, Mitsubishi, JVC,
RCA, Daewoo, Philips, Samsung, Sharp, and Toshiba. Mike was, to put it
mildly, overwhelmed. He went by the library and read what *Consumer
Reports* had to say about the various sets. Then he went online and read
reviews by users. The more he read, the more confused he became. After
spending more than 20 hours over three weekends pondering his options,
Mike decided to wait. "This is a major decision. I don't want to make any

mistakes. I got overwhelmed with information and choices. I'm going to take some time to think this over."

There's nothing inherently wrong with Mike's decision to postpone buying a new TV. However, his dilemma provides us an opportunity to ponder whether this is *really* an important decision for Mike. A lot of people seem to get confused about what decisions are truly important and deserve careful analysis and those that may seem important, but, on closer examination, fail to pass the importance test.

What's the *importance test*? The importance of a decision increases in direct proportion to its effect on your future. A decision you make today that will shape your life 20 years from now is considerably more important than one whose influence will last only a few months.

Let's return to Mike's concern about buying a new television. Do you think that set will be influencing his life in 10 or 20 years? Probably not. Like many electronic products, most of us replace them before 10 years are up. If Mike makes a mistake and buys a TV he later regrets, the long-term implications are relatively minor. The difference in picture quality among all the sets he's looking at is relatively minor, and the quality of Mike's life is not likely to be adversely affected because he chose a 40-inch set rather than a 50-inch one.

What about a decision to buy a new car? Is this important? Most of us trade our cars every five or six years, so there are minimal long-term implications from a bad car choice. However, if you're buying a car and expect it to be the last car you ever buy, it might be an important decision for you.

So what are typical examples of important decisions? What are decisions that are life-changing and justify a detailed and thorough assessment? Dropping out of school. Having a child. Committing to drugs. Staying with a "go nowhere" job. Note how all of these can change your life. Also note that, for many people, these are decisions that are often made on the spur of the moment, with little or no thought to their long-term repercussions.

When you're 70 or 80 years old and looking back on the key decisions that shaped your life, they're unlikely to be related to choosing a computer, buying a car, or picking a vacation spot. However, lots of people spend a great deal of time worrying and analyzing about decisions such as these *and* fail to give the appropriate attention to those decisions that really make a difference. Some people obsess about the smallest decision. They're convinced that every decision is important. In business, we often call this "paralysis by analysis." You haven't enough time or energy to try to optimize every decision. And if you don't differentiate between critical decisions and the rest, you end up shortchanging the truly critical ones.

If you don't differentiate between critical decisions and the rest, you end up shortchanging the truly critical ones.

There is no universal standard that defines for every person what is or is not an important decision. A few choices—like quitting school early or becoming a parent—are probably life-changing for almost all of us, but each of us has to identify those decisions that are uniquely important.

Although I haven't found any formal method to help you identify important decisions, I suggest that the importance of certain types of decisions vary with your age. Here are some examples of important decisions, organized by age. These are decisions that, if not properly considered, can lead to serious negative life outcomes: poor health, financial distress, loneliness, boredom, broken family relations, low self-esteem, and/or lack of lifetime achievements. Keep in mind that these are only suggestions and, as generalizations, may not be appropriate for everyone:

- *Teen years.* Taking up smoking; using drugs; quitting school; choosing "bad" friends; having irresponsible sex; having a child; driving recklessly

- *20s and 30s.* Staying with a "go-nowhere" job; failing to build a marketable skill; getting married; failing to develop a long-term financial plan (including beginning to save toward retirement)

- *40s and 50s.* Switching careers; gaining a large amount of weight; avoiding regular physical exams; having any elective surgery; failing to develop multiple interests and hobbies

- *60s and up.* Failing to plan for how postretirement days will be spent

In summary, I've argued that all decisions are not equal. You need to define for yourself which decisions are important and which aren't. You then need to direct a higher proportion of your time and effort to the important ones.

Decision Tips

- Direct a higher proportion of your time and effort to important decisions.

- Important decisions are defined as ones that are life changing— those that have a direct effect on your long-term future.

- Life-changing decisions tend to vary with age.

Chapter Thirty-One

More Information Isn't Necessarily Better

*An overload of information leads
to information blackout. It does
not enrich, but impoverishes.*
—*P. Drucker*

Carl Cooper just finished a four-week summer program for elementary and secondary teachers who are moving into administrative positions as principals or assistant principals. Carl found the course extremely helpful. He gained new insights into topics like strategy, budgeting, organization design, interpersonal communication, and leadership. He felt he now had a much better understanding of what he'd face as principal of Roosevelt Junior High School. What he wasn't so sure about was if he could apply all the new "stuff" he'd learned. "I'm a bit overwhelmed with all the new administrative concepts that we were taught."

We often hear that we live in the information age, and this new age can come with information overload. That is, the information we receive exceeds our capacity to process it. One of the more important research findings related to information processing was revealed nearly 50 years

137

ago. It says that the human memory imposes severe limitations on our ability to receive, process, and remember information; and that the number of unrelated pieces of information that the average person can retain is limited to about seven, plus or minus two.[1]

Let me state a list of 20 unrelated items. Read over the following list, then look away from this book, and see how many of them you can remember: aqua, couch, bread, Bosnia, giraffe, rental, voting, tonic, ring, hemline, radio, sweater, ears, vacation, wishful, quotation, redundant, case, club, pajamas. My best guess is that you were able to recall no more than five to nine of the items. We have a finite capacity for processing data. When the information we have to work with exceeds our processing capacity, the result is information overload.

We are continually bombarded with information. Radio, television, newspapers, books, magazines, the Internet, telephones, friends, relatives, and experts of all sorts envelope our eyes and ears with more and more information. No matter where you are—whether you're standing in New York's Times Square, walking through a supermarket, filling your car up with gas, or sitting in your living room—your senses are being attacked. And some of this is being filtered in, through your senses, to be used later for making decisions.

Quantity of information, however, is not synonymous with quality. Much of what you take in provides little in terms of giving you valid and reliable information from which to make judgments. When we experience information overload, we tend to select out, ignore, pass over, or forget information. Or we may put off further processing until the overload situation is over. Regardless, we lose information. It would be nice if we just lost the unimportant stuff. Unfortunately, we often lose valuable information from memory and end up recalling information that's irrelevant or biased. For instance, as we noted earlier in this book, information that evokes emotions, is particularly vivid, or that has occurred most recently is more likely to be recalled.

In the making of complex decisions, we often seek out more information because we associate *more* with *better*.[2] Again, as noted in previous chapters, the continual search for more information can result in needless delays or even complete inertia. Think of a pistol shooter who goes "ready, aim, aim, aim, aim. . ." and can't pull the trigger. When you're fearful of making a decision, it's easy to rationalize postponement by arguing that you need more information to make an intelligent decision.

The effective decision maker learns to know when enough is enough. He or she is also able to differentiate quality from quantity. Here are a few suggestions to help you with this task. Begin with focusing on your goals. I've said this numerous times before, but it's worth repeating: Clear

> *In the making of complex decisions, we often seek out more information because we associate* more *with* better.

goals are critical for rational decision making. If your goals are clear and consistent, you're less likely to keep searching for useless information, and you'll be better equipped to assess quickly whether new information is important or not. Second, accept that you're almost never going to have all the information you want to make a decision. Uncertainty is a part of life and a part of decision making. You can't eliminate uncertainty; you just want to acquire an appropriate amount of information to minimize it. Third, take time to think critically and reflect. Although you'll tend to keep your decision criteria and options to about seven, you're not limited to your immediate memory. Write things down. For important and complex decisions, use spreadsheet software to identify alternatives and to analyze them. And take time to reflect. Have you ever been working on a crossword puzzle, gotten stuck, walked away, and then come back to find you now have the answer? More and better choices often come from taking a break from the task at hand and returning to it at another time when your mind is in a different place. Finally, what defines an appropriate amount of information? What is "enough"? It's that point when you're able to conclude that further search is unlikely to generate any additional promising alternatives. At this point, you will have a full range of options and at least one that will provide you with a satisfactory choice. If you're still unsure, it can sometimes help to ask yourself this question: Would the additional time and effort necessary to develop more options provide that much better of a choice to justify that expenditure of time and effort?

Decision Tips

- Focus on goals.

- Accept that you'll never have all the information you want.

- Take time to think critically and to reflect.

- Make your final choice when additional effort no longer generates promising alternatives.

Don't Rehash Past Decisions

Whenever I make a bum decision,
I just go out and make another.
—H. Truman

J ulie Hernandez can drive herself nuts reliving her past decisions. "What if I had married Eddie, back in 2001, when he asked me? I think I should have started a savings program as soon as I got out of school rather than waiting until I was nearly 30. I think I bought too much life insurance. Maybe I should have waited a couple of more months and bought a more powerful computer."

Julie is full of "coulda, woulda, shoulda's." She seems to have no problem making decisions, but, regardless of how they turn out, she rehashes them over and over. She's also always second-guessing if she made the right decision originally.

Julie is not unique. A lot of us spend considerable time revisiting old decisions and second-guessing what might have been had we chosen another option. In some cases, rehashing past decisions can be functional.

However, more often than not, it's a waste of time and creates additional dysfunctional outcomes.

What's the plus side of revisiting past decisions? It can provide learning opportunities. We *can* learn from our past mistakes and successes. We learn what works and what doesn't. However, there is a large downside. It wastes time and effort. Remember from Chapter 22, after a decision is made, it's often a sunk cost. It can also make us gun-shy about making future decisions. Obsessing on past decisions has been linked to inertia and procrastination if we become fearful of making mistakes.[1]

The psychological concept we're talking about here is called *regret*. It's a negative emotion that we experience when we realize or imagine that our present situation would have been better had we made a previous decision differently.[2] We've all regretted, at one time or another, past decisions we've made. But some people seem to do it a lot more than others. You should be concerned about the negative side of regret because it lessens your decision effectiveness when you waste time "crying over spilt milk" and, more important, when it hinders your ability to make future decisions.

> *We've all regretted, at one time or another, past decisions we've made. But some people seem to do it a lot more than others.*

We know quite a bit about regret. For instance, to experience postdecision regret, you need to know the outcome of the decision you made.[3] If you buy a gift for someone and you never hear back as to whether or not they liked it, it's hard to experience regret. Moreover, you're more likely to experience regret when you know the outcomes for the alternatives you rejected. An acquaintance of mine continually relives his decision, made back in the late 1960s when he was living in Eugene, Oregon, to pass on an offer to invest in an upstart running-shoe business. That business became Nike. My acquaintance still regularly watches the price of Nike stock and "beats himself up" for his decision. While contrary to the previous example, the evidence also demonstrates that we tend to feel greater regret for actions we've taken than for inactions when a decision turns out badly.[4] People who start businesses and fail, for instance, are likely to focus on the belief that they would have been better off had they never pursued the business venture in the first place.

One of the most interesting and counterintuitive findings related to regret is that there are situations when people who are objectively more successful than someone else actually end up feeling worse than that other person. Specifically, it was found that athletes who finished second in the Olympic Games were less happy with their achievement than those who finished third.[5] The reason? The bronze medalists tended to focus more on fourth place and were thrilled to simply have earned a medal. In contrast, the silver medalists focused on the fact that they lost the gold and how close they were to being the Olympic champion.

When are you likely to experience regret? Four conditions have been proposed.[6] First, as mentioned previously, feedback has to be present. Regret is related to feelings that arise from comparing alternatives chosen with those rejected. If you don't know how a decision you made turned out, it's hard to experience regret. Second are situations where the alternative chosen is roughly equal in attractiveness to one or more other alternatives. If the alternative chosen turns out badly, it's easy to conclude that the wrong choice was made. This suggests that the more difficult a decision is, the more likely it is that you'll take regret into account when deciding. Third, you're likely to experience regret when the outcome from the decision will be quickly known. You're much more likely to regret not having looked when stepping off the curb into traffic, being hit by a car, and having to wear a leg cast for a month than you are to regret taking up smoking. The negative consequences from smoking are typically delayed by years or decades. And fourth, the more irreversible a decision is, the more likely you are to engage in regret if things go awry. Conversely, if you can easily correct a past mistake, you're less likely to experience regret about your previous choice.

You can't eliminate regret, but you can minimize it. All decisions, for instance, don't require follow-up. If you thoroughly researched the purchase of a new camera on the Internet and bought one, continuing your research after you placed the order isn't necessary, and it's likely to increase regret. Life's decisions come with enough feedback. You don't have to subject yourself to more if the decision is a sunk cost. You should devote more time to important decisions where several options are equally attractive. These are ones you're most likely to regret. Finally, devote more time to decisions that are irreversible.

Decision Tips

- All decisions don't require follow-up.

- Devote more time to important decisions where several options are equally attractive.

- Devote more time to decisions that are irreversible.

Chapter Thirty-Three

Successful People Take Risks

You miss 100 percent of the shots you never take.

—W. Gretzky

What do Bill Gates, Oprah Winfrey, Rudy Guiliani, Jerry Seinfeld, Ted Turner, Dolly Parton, Colin Powell, Donald Trump, and Pablo Picasso have in common? In addition to successful careers, they all took risks. If you're looking for one characteristic that differentiates people who have achieved great success from those who haven't, you would find that the successful people have taken a risk. They quit a job; they moved to a new city; they started a business; they ran for political office. They did something that made themselves vulnerable and exposed themselves to failure. I'm not proposing that risk taking *guarantees* success. Clearly, it doesn't. What I am saying is that it's very hard to become successful without giving up some security and taking a chance. As someone once said, "Behind every successful person was a mother who was convinced her kid was making a *huge* mistake."

Take a look back at your risk-taking score in Chapter 5. How did you rate? Risk taking is a personality factor. We all don't have the same tolerance for risk. If you scored low on risk taking, pay particular attention to this chapter and its recommendations. By actively trying to be more risk taking, you may be able to make more effective decisions. If you scored high on risk taking in Chapter 5, taking risks is already attractive to you. You need to be careful not to throw caution to the wind and seek out decision alternatives with oversized risks—choices where the downside losses far outweigh the upside potential.

It's very hard to become successful without giving up some security and taking a chance.

The easy route in life is to "stay the course" and not "make waves." This typically means making decisions that provide predictable outcomes and minimal threats to your known world: staying in the town you grew up in; keeping the same job for your entire career; going to your "regular" vacation spot every year; maintaining constant hobbies and interests; and the like. The low-risk life is often characterized by an appearance of a lack of decision making. Although you saw in Chapter 28 that choosing not to decide is still a decision, low risk takers are unlikely to see it that way. They think that, by minimizing change, they minimize risk. Low risk takers are also likely to be the same people who, when they reach their later years, look back disappointedly and wonder how they got to their current life state. Rather than actively manage their life, they passively sat on the sidelines and let life happen to them.

What do we know about risk taking and decision making? Here are a few highlights. High risk takers make quick decisions, but they're also deliberate.[1] Consistent with popular beliefs, high risk takers use less time to reach a decision and use less information. However, and this is counterintuitive, they tend to process each item of information more slowly. Therefore, although high risk takers may reach rapid decisions and restrict their information search, they give careful attention to the information they do acquire. Risk taking has also been found to change with age.[2] In comparing risk-taking propensity among people between ages 22 and 58, researchers found that both risk taking and the value placed upon risk was negatively related to age. That is, as we get older, we tend to become more conservative toward assuming risk. This is probably because older individuals perceive themselves as having more to lose. Finally, one of the most well-supported findings regarding risk taking and decision making (and mentioned previously in Chapter 18) is that we tend to evaluate outcomes differently depending on whether we're seeking to add to gains or to avert a loss.[3] We tend to be risk *averse* when we're looking at gains and risk *seeking* when facing losses. We seem to be particularly willing to take on unduly high risks in order to recoup or avoid losses. Stockholders, for instance, tend to sell winners too early and hold on to losers too long.[4] When an investment has gained in value, we often pass up future possible gains by getting out too quickly. Conversely, when a stock has fallen in value, we often hope for an upturn and risk further loss rather than accepting the certain loss.[5]

This chapter is predominantly directed at people who are risk averse. I've tried to demonstrate the downside of resisting change and being overconservative. With that said, I am not proposing that you take a gambling approach to decision making. Risk taking needs to be undertaken thoughtfully, intelligently, selectively, and with careful consideration of probabilities. Alternatives with minimal chances of success, regardless of payoffs, are gambles. However, you don't want to miss opportunities with good chances of success just because they have potential for failure.

The message of this chapter is threefold. First, embrace change. Change is not always a threat. It's often an opportunity—an opportunity with risk but, nevertheless, an opportunity. Second, know your risk tolerance and use this information to choose alternatives that are right for your level of risk seeking. And third, take *calculated* risks. Don't gamble. Carefully consider both the upside and downside potential from a decision. More important, recognize that, if you're risk averse, you're probably overweighing the downside. Even worst-case scenarios are often not as bad as they first appear.

Decision Tips

- Embrace change.

- Know your risk tolerance.

- Take calculated risks.

It's OK to Make Mistakes, or No One Has an Undefeated Season

The greatest mistake you can make in life is to be continually fearing you will make a mistake.

—E.G. Hubbard

Beethoven's music teacher once said of him that "as a composer, he is hopeless." Louisa May Alcott, author of *Little Women*, was told by an editor that she'd never write anything that people would like. A newspaper editor fired Walt Disney because he supposedly had no good ideas. Henry Ford's first business, the Detroit Automobile Company, failed within two years. His second automobile business also failed. However, his third, the Ford Motor Company, made him one of America's richest men. Steven Spielberg dropped out of high school in his sophomore year, and, when he was persuaded to come back, school officials placed him in a learning-disabled class. And arguably the greatest basketball player of all time, Michael Jordan, was cut from his high school basketball team.[1]

The previous examples illustrate the point of this chapter. Some of the most accomplished people have faced setbacks and failures. However, when people view them as learning opportunities and extract insights from them, they can be used to improve future decision making.

> *It's up to you to decide whether you will treat your mistakes as failures or as new information to learn from.*

This chapter is an extension of our previous discussion of risk taking. The greater the risks you take, the greater the probability that you'll make mistakes. It's up to you to decide whether you will treat your mistakes as failures or as new information to learn from.

Two streams of research can provide us with insights into how and why we respond the way we do to mistakes and setbacks. These are reinforcement theory and studies on perfectionism.

Reinforcement theory tells us that repeated failures lessen our motivation to try again.[2] Take, for instance, your current interests and hobbies. You probably continue them because you're relatively good at them. If you spend your spare time knitting, golfing, reading, doing crossword puzzles, drawing, or building computers, I'd predict that part of the reason you enjoy the activity you've chosen is that you're relatively successful at it. Now think about activities you've tried and never gone back to. My guess is that you had no natural talent for the activity or that you found the activity difficult, so you lacked motivation to continue or to develop your skill. We all have a tendency to want to repeat those activities where we're positively reinforced with successes or successive improvements and to avoid activities where there is no positive reinforcement. What does this mean in terms of decision making? You're going to make choices that don't turn out as you expected, and these setbacks are likely to make it more difficult for you to make future decisions that encompass uncertainty and risk.

Another barrier to accepting mistakes is the desire for perfectionism. A number of us are perfectionists—meaning we have a strong desire to do well at tasks and also tend to resist short-term change.[3] Although perfectionism is a complex concept, its major dimension is excessive concern over making mistakes.[4] People high in *perfectionism* fear failing, making mistakes, and losing control.[5] They are also more likely to be plagued by procrastination.[6] It appears that a perfectionist's response to the fear of making a mistake is often to avoid making decisions. If you have strong perfectionist tendencies, beware that this can lead to both fear of making mistakes and procrastination.

So how do you counteract the reinforcing pressures of setbacks? How can you move forward and not become "gun-shy" after you've made decisions that didn't work out as you had hoped? You begin by acknowledging that failures are part of life. Life is made up of uncertainties, so the only way to avoid failures is to avoid uncertainty and risk. Is that the kind of life you want to live? Probably not. What you need to do is to extract lessons from your setbacks. Given that you're going to make mistakes, what can you learn from them? What insights can they provide you that can help you make better decisions in the future? Making mistakes is OK; you just don't want to repeat the same mistakes. And once you make a mistake, you want to bounce back from it. The best way to do this is to seek out small victories. After a major setback, make decisions where you can achieve "small wins" or make small improvements. This will help you regain your confidence. As a case in point, a friend of mine decided to try to impress his girlfriend by cooking her an elaborate French-cuisine dinner. It was a disaster. None of the recipes turned out right. His first reaction was to give up his efforts at trying to prepare gourmet meals, but, on second thought, he decided to go for small wins. The next time he invited her over, he grilled steaks and focused his gourmet talents on the crème brûlée dessert.

Decision Tips

- Look for lessons in mistakes.

- If you're a perfectionist, be particularly alert to tendencies to procrastinate.

- Seek small successes or small improvements.

Chapter Thirty-Five

Experience Can Improve Decisions, but. . .

Experience is the name everyone gives to their mistakes.
—O. Wilde

A Cleveland, Ohio, fire commander and his crew encountered a fire at the back of a house. The commander led his hose team into the building. Standing in the living room, they blasted water onto the smoke and flames that appeared to consume the kitchen. But the fire roared back and continued to burn. The men doused the fire again, and the flames briefly subsided. Then they flared up again with an even greater intensity. As the firefighters retreated and regrouped, the commander was gripped by an uneasy feeling. He ordered everyone to leave. Just as the crew reached the street, the living-room floor caved in. Had the men stayed in the house, they would have plunged into a blazing basement.[1]

Why did the commander give the order to leave? Because the fire's behavior didn't match his expectations. Much of the fire was burning underneath the living-room floor, so it was unaffected by the firefighters' attack. Also, the rising heat made the room extremely hot—too hot for such a seemingly small fire. Another clue that this was not just a small kitchen fire was that the sounds it emitted were strangely quiet. Hot fires are loud. The commander was intuitively sensing that the floor was muffling the roar of the flames that were raging below.

Veteran firefighters have accumulated a storehouse of experiences, and they subconsciously categorize fires according to how they should react to them. They look for cues or patterns in situations that direct them to take one action over another. In other words, veteran firefighters use their experience to make better decisions.

As shown in the fire-fighting example, experience can be an excellent teacher. But not always! Experience can also lead to arrogance, overconfidence, and choices that lack creativity. For instance, if you scored high in Chapter 10 on overconfidence, you need to be careful not to let your experience cloud your objectivity and limit your choices. In this chapter, you'll look at situations where experience is a plus and where it can be a hindrance.

The common argument in favor of experience in decision making follows this logic. Over time, we make mistakes; we learn from those mistakes about what works and what doesn't; we gain experience; and that experience helps us to make better decisions in the future. Consistent with our discussion in the previous chapter, then, experience allows us to learn from our mistakes.

Before I proceed too far, let's clarify what I mean by the term *experience*. Is it age? Is it length of time doing an activity? Is it a measure of accumulated expertise? The value of experience in decision making is likely to depend on how you define the term.[2] Because we're concerned with both quality and quantity, we'll define experience to be repeated feedback that accumulates into developed expertise. Therefore, 20 years of "experience" may not reflect 20 years of accumulated expertise. It may merely be one year of experience repeated 20 times!

Many of the biases and errors described in Part III don't lessen with experience. This has been explained by pointing out three limitations to experience.[3] First, there is delay in feedback. Because there is typically a long lag time between making a decision and its outcome, it's often hard for people to learn from their mistakes. Second, people never know what the outcome would have been had they made another choice. So, learning is hampered by the lack of a clear cause-effect relationship. And third, there is variability between situations. Learning is clouded because we can't be sure that what worked (or didn't work) in one situation would achieve similar results in another situation. These limitations suggest that just because we know *what* happened (experience) doesn't mean we know *why* it happened (learning) and are able to act on our knowledge.[4]

The strongest case for experience is its value for assessing situations and in making routine decisions.[5] Experience allows you to size up a situation: "I've seen this situation a number of times before, and I know what's worked and what hasn't, so here's what I need to do." Experience also works well with routine situations because, again, past practices provide insights into how to best solve a problem. In the same way that organizations create rules and procedures so employees can quickly and efficiently solve routine problems, individuals create mental "programs" for handling recurring problems. For instance, you drive to work every day using the interstate highway. Each morning, just before you leave home, you check the traffic report. On those days when there's an accident and traffic is backed up, you take an alternate route that's two miles longer, but that you've learned is never congested.

What about the downside of experience? Experience can reduce decision quality when it leads to arrogance, overconfidence, or inaccurate perceptions, or when it limits creativity. As noted in Chapter 12, overconfidence can be a problem for all of us. But it's more likely to seriously undermine

> *Experience can reduce decision quality when it leads to arrogance, overconfidence, and inaccurate perceptions, or when it limits creativity.*

decision quality when it's applied in a different context or when conditions change. Paul Allen became one of the richest men in the world by cofounding Microsoft. Yet that expertise hasn't proved transferable to his Vulcan Ventures—where he's lost billions of dollars in an assortment of investments related to trying to create a wired world. Experience can also lead to inaccurate perceptions.[6] We see what we expect to see, and extensive experience can limit our perceptions. If your experiences are biased, your perceptions are likely to be inaccurate. So, you can misperceive problems, possible solutions, and the risks associated with various solutions. Finally, experience can limit creativity.[7] With new and novel decisions that require innovative solutions, experience can reduce your ability to see "outside the box." Many important scientific breakthroughs and inventions, in fact, have been made by naïve individuals who didn't know enough to know that it couldn't be done!

My conclusion? Be aware that experience can be a liability as well as an asset. It can lead to arrogance and overconfidence. Individuals who have had success in the past need to be especially alert not to behave overconfidently, especially when dealing with problems that are outside their areas of expertise. You should also be cautious about relying on your experience when dealing with new and novel situations. Finding a creative solution will require you to think outside your normal range of options. However, you should feel comfortable relying on your experience when dealing with routine problems.

Decision Tips

- Be aware that experience can lead to arrogance and overconfidence.
- Downplay experience in new and novel situations that require innovative solutions.
- Rely on experience with routine problems.

Chapter Thirty-Six

Where You're from Influences How You Decide

When in Rome,
do as the Romans do.
—St. Ambrose

Except for vacations to Canada and Mexico, Chris Reed had never been out of the United States. That changed with his recent assignment in Saudi Arabia. Since joining ExxonMobil as a geologist in 1998, Chris had spent all his time in Texas. Now his company has him heading up its exploration team on a $15 billion natural gas project in South Ghawar.

Chris has quickly learned that he's not in Midland, Texas, anymore. "People here are very different, and it's hard to adjust," Chris says. "The company provides us with all the amenities of home, so I have nothing to complain about with my accommodations. But the Saudis I work with aren't at all like my coworkers were back in Texas. Trust is very important in interactions with Saudis. In the U.S., we rely less on trust and more on contracts and legal documents. Saudis also seem to worry a lot about how a decision outcome will reflect on their family. That's not a very big concern back home. And people here put a great emphasis on honor. You don't want to cause an Arab to lose face. Dignity and reputation are very important. But probably nothing has been harder to adjust to than the

157

Saudi's approach to time. Unlike Americans, they have great patience. Saudis are very flexible when it comes to time and schedules. Decision deadlines have little meaning to them. I'm told it has something to do with their culture's pattern of fatalism." [1]

We are all products of the culture in which we were raised, and cultures differ. Studies indicate that cultures vary along a number of dimensions, for example, assertiveness, future orientation, and individualism versus collectivism. [2] Americans, for instance, are more assertive than Swedes, more future oriented than Russians, and more individualistic than the Japanese. In many Middle Eastern countries, people see life as essentially preordained (per Chapter 6, they would have high external locus of control scores). When something happens, they tend to see it as "God's will." In contrast, Americans and Canadians believe they can control nature. Western cultures also perceive time as a scarce resource. Because "time is money," it needs to be used efficiently. So Americans, as a case in point, obsess with making and keeping appointments and are enamored with time-saving devices—such as day planners, overnight mail delivery, cell phones, appliances with automatic timers, and remote control devices. Most people from Middle Eastern and Latin American countries don't share this fixation with time and schedules that is so prevalent in North America.

The message of this chapter is that culture shapes decision making. Although there are many aspects of decision making affected by culture, I'll limit my discussion to just a few. Let's look at how culture influences problem solvability, rationality and consistency, goals, and risk propensity.

Some cultures emphasize solving problems, while others focus on accepting situations as they are. The United States falls in the former category; Thailand and Indonesia fall into the latter. Thais, for instance, may be slower to identify a problem and more reluctant to initiate change than their British or American counterparts.

The rational process described in Chapter 2 makes no acknowledgement of cultural differences. Although rationality is valued in North America, Western Europe, and some other parts of the world, we can't generalize around the globe. In the United States, for instance, a good decision is arrived at by ensuring that it is consistent with a person's goals. To achieve that end, Americans are encouraged to set clear goals, identify all viable alternatives, to carefully and thoughtfully evaluate those alternatives, and to select the choice that best optimizes the goals. However, in countries such as Iran, where rationality is not deified, a good decision is likely to be made intuitively and to be judged against its alignment with Islamic tenants. In some parts of the world, spirituality, religion, or superstition are the driving forces behind making choices—not rationality.

Cultural differences—specifically collectivism versus individualism—shape willingness to take risks. For instance, the Chinese have been found to be more risk seeking than Americans, particularly on investment decisions.[3] Why? This seems to be the result of the fact that people in collectivist countries, like China, are more likely to receive financial help

> *Don't assume people from other countries make decisions the same way you do and don't assume that, because their decision process differs from yours, it is somehow inferior.*

from family members and relatives if they suffer a setback. If your culture provides a broader safety net, you're more willing to take daring risks.

The dominant decision-making style and practices in any given country reflect that country's national culture. Therefore, the process that defines a good decision in Canada may not be considered appropriate in China. As a result, don't assume people from other countries make decisions the same way you do and don't assume that, because their decision process differs from yours, it is somehow inferior. Although rationality is idealized in decision-making theory, this theory is culturally biased because most research and writing on the subject has been conducted by people from countries where goals and consistency are valued—like the United States, Canada, Western Europe, and Israel. Where good decision making is not judged by rationality, you should adjust your practices to reflect what *is* valued.

Decision Tips

- Don't assume people from other countries make decisions the same way you do.

- Although rationality is idealized in decision-making theory, it is culturally biased.

- Where good decision making is not judged by rationality, adjust your practices to reflect what *is* valued.

An Epilogue

Summary
or
Why Ignorance Isn't Bliss

When you get to the fork
in the road, take it!
—Y. Berra

Y ou've covered a lot of ground in this book. You've learned about the concept of rational decision making and why it's so hard to be rational. You took seven personality tests and considered what your scores mean in terms of how you make decisions. You read about more than a dozen biases and errors that many of us make in the decision process. For instance, we tend to be overconfident, we rely on the most available information rather than the most important, we limit our alternatives, and we finish our search too soon. Decision Tips were included to help you overcome these biases and errors. Finally, you read a number of suggestions—many of them counterintuitive—that can make you a better decision maker.

What should you walk away with after having read this book? The following summary points capture the essence of what you should have gotten from this book.

• **You can improve your decision making**

No skill may be more important to success in life than the ability to make competent decisions. Although most people have had little or no formal training in developing this skill, there is a substantive body of knowledge that can help you make better decisions. This book has attempted to bring that knowledge to you. This book's major contention has been that you can improve your decision making. I've presented the major obstacles and provided suggestions for overcoming those obstacles.

> *No skill may be more important to success in life than the ability to make competent decisions.*

The focus has been on the decision process rather than outcomes. That's because a good decision should be judged by the process used, not the results achieved. Unfortunately, in some situations, you'll find that a "good decision" results in an undesirable outcome. If you used the right process, however, you will have made a good decision regardless of the outcome.

Learning to use the right process is not an easy task. It will require considerable work on your part. Many of the bad habits you currently have were developed over decades. Replacing them with good habits won't happen overnight. Follow the guidelines presented in this book, and reread this book every once in a while to remind yourself where you can improve.

• **It all starts with goals**

No theme reappears in this book more often than the importance of goals. Everything evolves from goals. Without them, you can't be rational, you can't differentiate important decisions from unimportant ones, you don't know what information you need, you don't know which information is relevant and which is irrelevant, you'll find it difficult to choose between alternatives, and you're far more likely to experience regret over the choices you make.

You need long-term goals and short-term ones. You also need a plan or road map that can get you from where you are to where you want to be. If your goals are clear, you'll be amazed at how much easier it is to make decisions. You'll be able to quickly eliminate options that are inconsistent with your interests, and you'll significantly reduce the likelihood that you'll make choices that take you in directions that you'll later regret.

• Use the rational process whenever possible

The goal of effective decision making is to be as rational as possible. And you're rational when you seek to make consistent and value-maximizing choices within the constraints you're given.

The rational decision process follows six steps: (1) Identify and define the problem; (2) Identify decision criteria; (3) Weight the criteria; (4) Generate alternatives; (5) Evaluate each alternative; (6) Select the choice that scores highest.

Although these steps seem straightforward and relatively easy to implement, they're not—especially with complex decisions. Biases, personality tendencies, and bad habits all get in the way.

Do you always need to be consistent? No. When you obsess on consistency, you create barriers to change. Although most First-World societies value consistency and look askew at behavior that is inconsistent, sometimes flexibility can also be an asset. It's alright to be inconsistent if you can objectively justify it. Conditions change. What was an appropriate decision last week or last year, because of changing conditions, may no longer be the best choice. Your previous decision may not necessarily have been wrong; it just may no longer fit the prior conditions it was made under. Continuing down the wrong path merely to maintain the appearance of consistency is foolhardy.

• There are costs in doing nothing

When faced with a tough or complex decision, a natural response for many of us is to do nothing. This seems to come from the assumptions that it's always better to err on the side of caution and that the cost of delay is minimal or nothing. However, I've argued strongly that the decision to do nothing is still a decision. It's a decision to maintain the status quo.

To the degree that the status quo is a desirable state, "staying the course" comes at a minimal price. It's when this approach is taken in order to avoid having to deal with hard choices that it can become a serious handicap.

Challenge yourself to directly question the status quo. To ensure that you're not becoming too comfortable with your current situation or too fearful of the consequences from making changes, you need occasionally to ask yourself this question: Why shouldn't I pursue another path from the one I'm currently on? By shifting the frame from one of "why *should* I change?" to "why *shouldn't* I change?," you become proactive and increase the probability of addressing problems before they become serious.

• Know your personality tendencies

It's been said, tongue in cheek, that "you're unique, just like everyone else!" Ironically, there is some truth in this statement. Each of us *is* unique, but we're unique in similar ways. Trait theorists, for instance, have identified primary personality characteristics that are common among all individuals, but along which people differ to a degree. For instance, risk tolerance is a personality trait, and people differ in their willingness to assume risk.

In Part II of this book, you took short tests for seven personality factors: decision style, risk tolerance, locus of control, procrastination, impulsiveness, emotional control, and overconfidence. Although these are not the only important personality factors that influence decision making, they do provide some valuable insights into how you approach and make decisions. For example, your score on locus of control offers insights into the degree to which you believe that your decision choices can actually shape your destiny. And your score on impulsiveness suggests how likely you are to make decisions on the spur of the moment and focus on the present rather than the future.

You should use this personality feedback to better understand your tendencies and to make adjustments when these tendencies might hinder your decision effectiveness.

• Look for information that disconfirms your beliefs

One of the most effective means for counteracting overconfidence, the confirmation bias (seeking out information that reaffirms our past choices), and the hindsight bias (falsely believing we'd have accurately predicted the outcome of an event, after that outcome is actually known) is to actively look for information that contradicts our beliefs and assumptions. When we overtly consider various ways we could be wrong, we challenge our tendencies to think we're smarter than we actually are. In effect, we become our own devil's advocate by assuming our beliefs are wrong and by aggressively searching out alternative explanations. If our beliefs are correct, they'll stand up under close inspection. If they're flawed, this approach is likely to reveal it.

• Consider how an impartial outsider might see a situation differently

It's hard to see situations differently when we look through our biased lenses. Our attitudes, motives, expectations, interests, prejudices, and past experiences cloud our objectivity. A successful way for dealing with these biases is to stand away from the situation and look at it from an impartial outsider's perspective. Put yourself in someone else's shoes, someone who isn't emotionally involved in the decision and who doesn't necessarily see it through your prior decisions and commitments, likes and dislikes, frames, and so on. For important decisions, you should also consider getting others' advice. Input from a neutral party can often offer insights and perspectives that you're unable to provide.

• Don't try to create meaning out of random events

The educated mind has been trained to look for cause-effect relations. When something happens, we ask why. Although such thinking is obviously desirable, it has a downside. When things happen by chance, we tend to look for reasons. And when we can't find reasons, we often create them out of thin air.

We like to believe we have some control over our world and destiny, but the truth is that the world will always contain random events. You need to be able to accept this fact, differentiate chance events from those that actually follow established patterns, and avoid trying to create meaning out of random data.

You have to accept that there are events in life that are outside your control. Ask yourself if patterns can be meaningfully explained or whether they are merely coincidence. Don't attempt to create meaning out of coincidence.

• Increase your options

When it comes to assessing decision alternatives, my advice is the more the merrier. No matter how many options you've identified, your final choice can be no better than the best of the option set you've selected. This argues for increasing your options and for using creativity in developing a wide range of diverse choices.

Even if an obvious alternative looks perfect, you have to resist your tendency to choose it quickly and conclude the decision process. Keep searching to expand your set of alternatives. More important, be creative in your search for alternatives. Look "outside the box" to consider strange, unconventional, and previously untried options. The more alternatives you can generate, and the more diverse those alternatives, the greater your chance of finding an outstanding one.

• It's OK to make mistakes

When you're afraid to make mistakes, you miss learning opportunities. You also tend to avoid active decisions—either doing nothing for fear of failure or making choices only when you're forced into it. And if you're afraid to make mistakes, you won't take risks. Instead, you'll go for the safe choices.

In many cases, the safe choice is the best choice, but it isn't always. I'm not advocating arbitrary risk taking. Rather, you need to choose your risks thoughtfully, intelligently, selectively, and with careful consideration of probabilities. Alternatives with minimal chances of success, regardless of payoffs, are gambles. However, you don't want to miss opportunities with good chances of success just because they have potential for failure.

Here is a final thought. You have the power to control your future through the decisions you make. By understanding and practicing the suggestions we offered in this book, you can improve the processes by which you make choices and statistically increase your decision batting average. Ignorance isn't bliss. You can ignore the wealth of research insights summarized in this book. Or, you can start applying them today and become a more effective decision maker. The decision is yours!

End Notes

Chapter 2

1. See, for example, R. Hastie and R. M. Dawes, *Rational Choice in an Uncertain World: The Psychology of Judgment and Decision Making* (Thousand Oaks, CA: Sage, 2001), pp. 17–19; K. M. Galotti, *Making Decisions That Matter: How People Face Important Life Choices* (Mahwah, NJ: Erlbaum, 2002), pp. 3–4; and S. Williams, *Making Better Business Decisions* (Thousand Oaks, CA: Sage, 2002), pp. 5–15.

2. See H. A. Simon, "Rationality in Psychology and Economics," *Journal of Business* (October 1986), pp. 209–224; A. Langley, "In Search of Rationality: The Purposes Behind the Use of Formal Analysis in Organizations," *Administrative Science Quarterly* (December 1989), pp. 598–631; and G. Harman, "Rationality," in *An Invitation to Cognitive Science: Thinking*, 2nd ed., ed. D. N. Osherson (Cambridge, MA: MIT Press, 1995), pp. 175–211.

3. See E. F. Harrison, *The Managerial Decision-Making Process*, 4th ed. (Boston: Houghton Mifflin, 1995), pp. 2–7.

Chapter 3

1. This opening example on the risk of terrorism is based on M. Kinsley, "How to Live a Rational Life," *Time*, September 9, 2002, p. 88.

2. E. Shafir and R. A. LeBoeuf, "Rationality," in *Annual Review of Psychology*, vol. 53, eds S. T. Fiske, D. L. Schacter, and C. Zahn-Waxler (Palo Alto, CA: Annual Reviews, 2002), pp. 491–517.

3. J. G. March, *A Primer on Decision Making* (New York: Free Press, 1994), pp. 2–7; and D. Hardman and C. Harries, "How Rational Are We?" *Psychologist* (February 2002), pp. 76–79.

4. This section is based on R. J. Meyer and J. Wesley Hutchinson, "Bumbling Geniuses: The Power of Everyday Reasoning in Multistage Decision Making," in *Wharton on Making Decisions*, eds S. J. Hoch and H. C. Kunreuther (New York: Wiley, 2001), pp. 50–51; and H. A. Simon, *Administrative Behavior*, 3rd ed. (New York: Macmillan, 1976).

Chapter 4

1. This instrument is adapted from S. G. Scott and R. A. Bruce, "Decision-Making Style: The Development and Assessment of a New Measure," *Educational and Psychological Measurement* (October 1995), pp. 818-831. Reprinted by permission of Sage Publications. For additional support, see R. Loo, "A Psychometric Evaluation of the General Decision-Making Style Inventory," *Personality and Individual Differences* (November 2000), pp. 895–905.

2. See, for instance, J. C. Henderson and P. C. Nutt, "The Influence of Decision Style on Decision Making Behavior," *Management Science* (April 1980), pp. 371–86; and D. Keirsey, *Please Understand Me II* (Del Mar, CA: Prometheus Nemesis, 1998).

Chapter 5

1. Adapted from N. Kogan and M. A. Wallach, *Risk Taking: A Study in Cognition and Personality* (New York: Holt, Rinehart and Winston, 1964), pp. 256–61. Reprinted by permission.

Chapter 6

1. Adapted from J. B. Rotter, "External Control and Internal Control," *Psychology Today* (June 1971), p. 42. Reprinted by permission from *Psychology Today* magazine. Copyright c 1971 Sussex Publishers, Inc.

2. J. B. Rotter, "Generalized Expectancies for Internal versus External Control of Reinforcement," *Psychological Monographs* 80, no. 609 (1966).

Chapter 7

1. Adapted from M. Stainton, C. H. Lay, and G. L. Flett, "Trait Procrastinators and Behavior/Trait-Specific Cognitions," *Journal of Social Behavior and Personality* 15, no. 5 (2000), pp. 297–312. Reprinted with permission.

2. N. Milgram and R. Tenne, "Personality Correlates of Decisional and Task Avoidant Procrastination," *European Journal of Personality* (March–April 2000), p. 141.

3. Ibid., p. 142.

Chapter 8

1. Adapted from J. H. Patton, M. S. Stanford, and E. S. Barratt, "Factor Structure of the Barratt Impulsiveness Scale," *Journal of Clinical Psychology* (November 1995), p. 771. Reprinted by permission of John Wiley & Sons, Inc.

2. J. H. Patton, M. S. Stanford, and E. S. Barratt, "Factor Structure of the Barratt Impulsiveness Scale," 768–774.

3. Ibid.

Chapter 9

1. Based on M. Watson and S. Greer, "Development of a Questionnaire Measure of Emotional Control," *Journal of Psychosomatic Research* 27, no. 4 (1983), pp. 299–305. Reprinted with permission.

Chapter 10

1. Adapted from J. E. Russo and P. J. H. Schoemaker, *Decision Traps: Ten Barriers to Brilliant Decision Making and How to Overcome Them* (New York: Fireside, 1990). Reprinted by permission of Simon & Schuster.

2. J. E. Russo and P. J. H. Schoemaker, *Winning Decisions* (New York: Doubleday, 2002), p. 80.

3. Ibid., p. 78.

Chapter 12

1. S. Plous, *The Psychology of Judgment and Decision Making* (New York: McGraw Hill, 1993), p. 217.

2. S. Highhouse, "Judgment and Decision-Making Research: Relevance to Industrial and Organizational Psychology," in *Handbook of Industrial, Work & Organizational Psychology*, vol. 2, eds. N. Anderson et al (Thousand Oaks, CA: Sage, 2001), p. 320.

3. S. Lichtenstein and B. Fischhoff, "Do Those Who Know More Also Know More About How Much They Know?" *Organizational Behavior and Human Performance* (December 1977), pp. 159–183.

4. B. Fischhoff, P. Slovic, and S. Lichtenstein, "Knowing with Certainty: The Appropriateness of Extreme Confidence," *Journal of Experimental Psychology: Human Perception and Performance* (November 1977), pp. 552–564.

5. Cited in College Board, *Student Descriptive Questionnaire* (Princeton, NJ: Educational Testing Service, 1976–1977).

6. R. J. Burke, "Why Performance Appraisal Systems Fail," *Personnel Administration* (June 1972), pp. 32–40.

7. See, for instance, N. D. Weinstein, "Unrealistic Optimism About Future Life Events," *Journal of Personality and Social Psychology*

(November 1980), pp. 806–20; and "Economic Predictions: Personal Future Seems Brightest," *Psychology Today* (October 1989), p. 16.

8. J. E. Russo and P. J. H. Schoemaker, *Winning Decisions* (New York: Doubleday, 2002), p. 82.

9. M. H. Bazerman, *Judgment in Managerial Decision Making*, p. 100.

10. S. Plous, *The Psychology of Judgment and Decision Making*, p. 230.

11. J. Kruger and D. Dunning, "Unskilled and Unaware of It: How Difficulties in Recognizing One's Own Incompetence Lead to Inflated Self-Assessments," *Journal of Personality and Social Psychology* (November 1999), pp. 1,121-1,134.

12. B. Fischhoff, P. Slovic, and S. Lichtenstein, "Knowing with Certainty: The Appropriateness of Extreme Confidence."

13. These conclusions were based on J. E. Russo and P. J. H. Schoemaker, "Managing Overconfidence," *Sloan Management Review* (Winter 1992), pp. 11-12; and D. M. Messick and M. H. Bazerman, "Ethical Leadership and the Psychology of Decision Making," *Sloan Management Review* (Winter 1996), pp. 17–19.

14. A. Koriat, S. Lichtenstein, and B. Fischhoff, "Reasons for Confidence," *Journal of Experimental Psychology: Human Learning and Memory* (March 1980), pp. 107-118; and J. E. Russo and P. J. H. Schoemaker, "Managing Overconfidence," pp. 12–14.

15. "Zero-Defect Decision Making," *INC.*, March 2002, p. 117.

Chapter 13

1. N. Milgram and R. Tenne, "Personality Correlates of Decisional and Task Avoidant Procrastination," *European Journal of Personality* (March–April 2000), p. 141.

2. J. R. Ferrari, J. J. Johnson, and W. C. McCown, *Procrastination and Task Avoidance: Theory, Research, and Treatment* (New York: Plenum, 1995), p. 220.

3. See, for instance, G. Beswick, E. D. Rothblum, and L. Mann, "Psychological Antecedents of Student Procrastination," *Australian Psychologist* (July 1988), pp. 207–217; J. R. Ferrari and J. F. Dovidio, "Examining Behavioral Processes in Indecision: Decisional Procrastination and Decision-Making Style," *Journal of Research in Personality* (March 2000), pp. 127–137; and C. J. Anderson, "The Psychology of Doing Nothing: Forms of Decision Avoidance Result from Reason and Emotion," *Psychological Bulletin* (January 2003), pp. 139–67.

4. See I. L. Janis and L. Mann, *Decision Making: A Psychological Analysis of Conflict, Choice, and Commitment* (New York: Free Press, 1977); and A. Tversky and E. Shafir, "Choice Under Conflict: The Dynamics of Deferred Decision," *Psychological Science* (November 1992), pp. 358–61.

5. A. Tversky and E. Shafir, "Choice Under Conflict," p. 358

6. Ibid.

7. See O. E. Tykocinski, T. S. Pittman, and E. E. Tuttle, "Inaction Inertia: Foregoing Future Benefits as a Result of an Initial Failure to Act," *Journal of Personality and Social Psychology* (May 1995), p. 794.

8. N. Milgram and R. Tenne, "Personality Correlates of Decisional and Task Avoidant Procrastination," p. 142.

9. D. Ariely and K. Wertenbroch, "Procrastination, Deadlines, and Performance: Self-Control by Precommitment," *Psychological Science* (May 2002), pp. 219–24.

Chapter 14

1. Cited in D. Laibson, "A Debt Puzzle," at the Behavioral Economics Roundtable, Russell Sage Foundation Programs, October 8, 1999.

2. P. J. Lim, "Credit Squeeze," www.usnews.com, June 17, 2002.

3. See, for instance, T. O'Donoghue and M. Rabin, "The Economics of Immediate Gratification," *Journal of Behavioral Decision Making* (April/June 2000), pp. 233–250.

4. D. Goleman, *Emotional Intelligence* (New York: Bantam, 1995).

Chapter 15

1. See, for instance, A. Tversky and D. Kahneman, "Judgment Under Uncertainty: Heuristics and Biases," *Science* (September 1974), pp. 1,124–1,131.

2. J. S. Hammond, R. L. Keeney, and H. Raiffa, *Smart Choices* (Boston: HBS Press, 1999), p. 191.

3. R. Hastie, D. A. Schkade, and J. W. Payne, "Juror Judgments in Civil Cases: Effects of Plaintiff's Requests and Plaintiff's Identity on Punitive Damage Awards," *Law and Human Behavior* (August 1999), pp. 445-470.

4. G. B. Northcraft and M. A. Neale, "Experts, Amateurs, and Real Estate: An Anchoring-and-Adjustment Perspective on Property Pricing Decisions," *Organizational Behavior and Human Decision Processes* (February 1987), pp. 84–97.

5. T. Mussweiler and F. Strack, "Considering the Impossible: Explaining the Effects of Implausible Anchors," *Social Cognition* (April 2001), pp. 145–160.

6. S. Plous, *The Psychology of Judgment and Decision Making* (New York: McGraw, 1993), p. 152.

7. Ibid.

8. J. S. Hammond, R. L. Keeney, and H. Raiffa, *Smart Choices*, pp. 191–193.

Chapter 16

1. D. C. Dearborn and H. A. Simon, "Selective Perception: A Note on the Departmental Identification of Executives," *Sociometry* (June 1958), pp. 140–144.

2. R. P. Vallone, L. Ross, and M. R. Lepper, "The Hostile Media Phenomenon: Biased Perception and Perceptions of Media Bias in Coverage of the Beirut Massacre," *Journal of Personality and Social Psychology* (September 1985), pp. 577–585.

3. C. G. Lord, L. Ross, and M. R. Lepper, "Biased Assimilation and Attitude Polarization: The Effects of Prior Theories on Subsequently Considered Evidence," *Journal of Personality and Social Psychology* (November 1979), pp. 2,098–2,109.

Chapter 17

1. P. C. Wason, "On the Failure to Eliminate Hypotheses in a Conceptual Task," *Quarterly Journal of Experimental Psychology* (August 1960), pp. 129–40; R. S. Nickerson, "Confirmation Bias: A Ubiquitous Phenomenon in Many Guises," *Review of General Psychology* (June 1998), pp. 175–220; and E. Jonas, S. Schulz-Hardt, D. Frey, and N. Thelen, "Confirmation Bias in Sequential Information Search After Preliminary Decisions," *Journal of Personality and Social Psychology* (April 2001), pp. 557–571.

2. M. Bazerman, R. Beekun, and F. Schoorman, "Performance Evaluation in a Dynamic Context: A Laboratory Study of the Impact

of Prior Commitment to the Ratee," *Journal of Applied Psychology* (December 1982), pp. 873–876.

3. J. E. Russo and P. J. H. Schoemaker, *Winning Decisions* (New York: Doubleday, 2002), p. 84.

4. M. Lewicka, "Confirmation Bias: Cognitive Error or Adaptive Strategy of Action Control?" in *Personal Control in Action: Cognitive and Motivational Mechanisms*, eds. M. Kofta et al (New York: Plenum Press, 1998), pp. 233–58.

5. See, for instance, C. R. Mynatt, M. E. Doherty, and R. D. Tweney, "Consequences of Confirmation and Disconfirmation in a Simulated Research Environment," *Quarterly Journal of Experimental Psychology* (August 1978), pp. 395–406.

6. J. S. Hammond, R. L. Keeney, and H. Raiffa, *Smart Choices* (Boston: HBS Press, 1999), p. 200.

Chapter 18

1. I found this story retold in a number of places. For instance, see J. S. Hammond, R. L. Keeney, and H. Raiffa, *Smart Choices* (Boston: HBS Press, 1999), p. 200; and J. E. Russo and P. J. H. Schoemaker, *Winning Decisions* (New York: Random House, 2002), p. 39. The actual source is unknown.

2. See, for example, A. Tversky and D. Kahneman, "The Framing of Decisions and the Psychology of Choice," *Science* (January 1981), pp. 453–58; D. Frisch, "Reasons for Framing Effects," *Organizational Behavior and Human Decision Processes* (April 1993), pp. 399–429; and R.M. Entman, "Framing: Toward Clarification of a Fractured Paradigm," *Journal of Communication* (Autumn 1993), pp. 51–58.

3. J. E. Russo and P. J. H. Schoemaker, *Winning Decisions* (New York: Doubleday, 2002), p. 28.

4. Ibid., p. 37.

5. D. Kahneman and A. Tversky, "Prospect Theory: An Analysis of Decision Under Risk," *Econometrica* (March 1979), pp. 263–291.

6. D. K. Wilson, R. M. Kaplan, and L. J. Schneiderman, "Framing of Decisions and Selection of Alternatives in Health Care," *Social Behaviour* (March 1987), pp. 51–59.

Chapter 19

1. M. Memmott, "Fear May Be Overwhelming, but so Are the Odds," *USA Today*, October 18, 2002, p. 6A.

2. See A. Tversky and D. Kahneman, "Availability: A Heuristic for Judging Frequency and Probability," in *Judgment Under Uncertainty: Heuristics and Biases*, eds. D. Kahneman, P. Slovic, and A. Tversky (Cambridge: Cambridge Press, 1982), pp. 163–78.

Chapter 20

1. Cited in J. Simons, "Improbable Dreams," *U.S. News & World Report*, March 24, 1997, p. 46.

2. See D. Kahneman and A. Tversky, "On the Psychology of Prediction," *Psychological Review* (July 1973), pp. 251–73; and A. Tversky and D. Kahneman, "Judgment Under Uncertainty: Heuristics and Biases," *Sciences* (September 1974), pp. 1,124–1,131.

3. A. Tversky and D. Kahneman, "Belief in the Law of Small Numbers," *Psychological Bulletin* (August 1971), pp. 105–110.

4. M. B. O'Higgins, *Beating the Dow* (New York: HarperBusiness, 2000).

5. A. Tversky and D. Kahneman, "Judgment Under Uncertainty," p. 1,127.

Chapter 21

1. See, for instance, E. F. Fama, "Random Walks in Stock Market Prices," *Financial Analysts Journal* (September–October 1965), pp. 55–60.

2. B. Fischhoff and P. Slovic, "A Little Learning . . .: Confidence in Multicue Judgment Tasks," in *Attention and Performance*, vol. 8, ed. R. Nicherson (New Jersey: Erlbaum, 1980).

3. See, for example, N. Friedland, "Games of Luck and Games of Chance: The Effects of Luck-versus-Chance-Orientation on Gambling Decisions," *Journal of Behavioral Decision Making* (September 1998), pp. 161–179; and M. H. Guindon and F. J. Hanna, "Coincidence, Happenstance, Serendipity, Fate, or the Hand of God: Case Studies in Synchronicity," *Career Development Quarterly* (December 2001), pp. 195–208.

4. See , for instance, A. James and A. Wells, "Death Beliefs, Superstitious Beliefs and Health Anxiety," *British Journal of Clinical Psychology* (March 2002), pp. 43–53.

5. J. L. Bleak and C. M. Frederick, "Superstitious Behavior in Sport: Levels of Effectiveness and Determinants of Use in Three Collegiate Sports," *Journal of Sport Behavior* (March 1998), pp. 1–15.

Chapter 22

1. See, for instance, H. Arkes and C. Blumer, "The Psychology of Sunk Costs," *Organizational Behavior and Human Decision Processes* (February 1985), pp. 124–40; and R.L. Leahy, "Sunk Costs and Resistance to Change," *Journal of Cognitive Psychology* (Winter 2000), pp. 355–371.

2. H. Arkes and C. Blumer, "The Psychology of Sunk Costs."

3. B. M. Staw and H. Hoang, "Sunk Costs in the NBA: Why Draft Order Affects Playing Time and Survival in Professional Basketball," *Administrative Science Quarterly* (September 1995), pp. 474–494.

4. See, for instance, R. Hastie and R. M. Dawes, *Rational Choice in an Uncertain World* (Thousand Oaks, CA: Sage, 2001), pp. 36–45.

5. H-T. Tan and J. F. Yates, "Sunk Cost Effects: The Influences of Instruction and Future Return Estimates," *Organizational Behavior and Human Decision Processes* (September 1995), pp. 311–320.

6. K. Kroll, "Rising Above Sunk Costs," *Industry Week*, September 4, 2000, pp. 19–21.

Chapter 23

1. See, for instance, H. A. Simon, *Administrative Behavior*, 3rd ed. (New York: Macmillan, 1976); M. A. Goodrich, W. C. Stirling, and E. R. Boer, "Satisficing Revisited," *Minds & Machines* (February 2000), pp. 79–110; and D.E. Agosto, "Bounded Rationality and Satisficing in Young People's Web-Based Decision Making," *Journal of the American Society for Information Science and Technology* (January 2002), pp. 16–27.

2. J. Forester, "Bounded Rationality and the Politics of Muddling Through," *Public Administration Review* (January–February 1984), pp. 23–31; and G. Gigerenzer, ed., *Bounded Rationality: The Adaptive Toolbox* (Cambridge, MA: MIT Press, 2001).

3. L. R. Beach, *Image Theory: Decision Making in Personal and Organizational Contexts* (Chichester, England: Wiley, 1990); C. Seidl and S. Traub, "A New Test of Image Theory," *Organizational Behavior and Human Decision Processes* (August 1998), pp. 93–116; ed. L. R. Beach, *Image Theory: Theoretical and Empirical Foundations* (Mahwah, NJ: Erlbaum, 1998); and L. D. Ordonez, L. Benson III, and L.R. Beach, "Testing the Compatibility Test: How Instructions,

Accountability, and Anticipated Regret Affect Prechoice Screening of Options," *Organizational Behavior and Human Decision Processes* (April 1999), pp. 63–80.

Chapter 24

1. See, for instance, R. Plutchik, *The Psychology and Biology of Emotion* (New York: HarperCollins, 1994).

2. K. Fiedler, "Emotional Mood, Cognitive Style, and Behavioral Regulation," in *Affect, Cognition, and Social Behavior*, eds. K. Fiedler and J. Forgas (Toronto: Hogrefe Int., 1988), pp. 100–19; and T. Gilovich and V. H. Medvec, "The Experience of Regret: What, Why, and When," *Psychological Review* (April 1995), pp. 379–395.

3. G. Loewenstein, "Out of Control: Visceral Influences on Behavior," *Organizational Behavior and Human Decision Processes* (March 1996), pp. 272–292; and M. F. Luce, J. R. Bettman, and J. W. Payne, "Choice Processing in Emotionally Difficult Decisions," *Journal of Experimental Psychology: Learning, Memory, and Cognition* (March 1997), pp. 384–405.

4. M. der Hovanesian, "Master Your Market Mood Swings," *Business Week*, September 30, 2002, pp. 108–109.

Chapter 25

1. J. M. Schlesinger and B. Gruley, "A Tale of a Broker and His Clients and an Era's End," *Wall Street Journal*, December 27, 2002, p. A1.

2. D. T. Miller and M. Ross, "Self-Serving Biases in the Attribution of Causality: Fact or Fiction?" *Psychological Bulletin* (March 1975), pp. 213–225; B. Mullen and C.A. Riordan, "Self-Serving Attributions for Performance in Naturalistic Settings: A Meta-Analytic Review," *Journal of Applied Social Psychology* (January 1988), pp. 3–22; and N. Epley and D. Dunning, "Feeling 'Holier Than Thou': Are Self-

Serving Assessments Produced by Errors in Self- or Social Prediction?" *Journal of Personality and Social Psychology* (December 2000), pp. 861–875.

3. H. Seneviratne and B. Saunders, "An Investigation of Alcohol Dependent Respondents' Attributions for Their Own and Others' Relapses," *Addiction Research* (October 2000), pp. 439–453.

Chapter 26

1. B. Fischhoff and R. Beyth, "'I Knew It Would Happen': Remembered Probabilities of Once-Future Things," *Organizational Behavior and Human Performance* (February 1975), pp. 1–16; S. A. Hawkins and R. Hastie, "Hindsight: Biased Judgments of Past Events After the Outcomes Are Known," *Psychological Bulletin* (May 1990), pp. 311–27; J. J. J. Christensen-Szalanski, "The Hindsight Bias: A Meta-Analysis," *Organizational Behavior and Human Decision Processes* (February 1991), pp. 147–168; and L. Werth, F. Strack, and J. Foerster, "Certainty and Uncertainty: The Two Faces of the Hindsight Bias," *Organizational Behavior and Human Decision Processes* (March 2002), pp. 323–341.

2. J. M. Bonds-Raacke, L. S. Fryer, S. D. Nicks, and R. T. Durr, "Hindsight Bias Demonstrated in the Prediction of a Sporting Event," *Journal of Social Psychology* (June 2001), pp. 349–352.

3. See, for instance, E. Erdfelder and A. Buckner, "Decomposing the Hindsight Bias: A Multinomial Processing Tree Model for Separating Recollection and Reconstruction in Hindsight," *Journal of Experimental Psychology: Learning, Memory, and Cognition* (March 1998), pp. 387–414.

4. F. B. Bryant and R. L. Guilbault, "'I Knew It All Along' Eventually: The Development of Hindsight Bias in Reaction to the Clinton

Impeachment Verdict," *Basic and Applied Social Psychology* (March 2002), pp. 27–41.

5. B. Fischhoff, "Perceived Informativeness of Facts," *Journal of Experimental Psychology: Human Perception and Performance* (May 1977), pp. 349–358.

6. P. Slovic and B. Fischhoff, "On the Psychology of Experimental Surprises," *Journal of Experimental Psychology: Human Perception and Performance* (November 1977), pp. 544–551.

Chapter 27

1. R.J. Meyer and J. W. Hutchinson, "Bumbling Geniuses: The Power of Everyday Reasoning in Multistage Decision Making," in *Wharton on Making Decisions*, eds S. J. Hoch and H. C. Kunreuther (New York: Wiley, 2001), p. 44.

2. Ibid., pp. 46-47.

3. A. Tversky and E. Shafir, "Choice Under Conflict: The Dynamics of Deferred Decision," *Psychological Science* (November 1992), p. 358.

Chapter 28

1. O. E. Tykocinski, T. S. Pittman, and E. E. Tuttle, "Inaction Inertia: Foregoing Future Benefits as a Result of an Initial Failure to Act," *Journal of Personality and Social Psychology* (May 1995), pp. 793–803.

2. T. Gilovich and V. H. Medvec, "The Experience of Regret: What, Why, and When," *Psychological Review* (April 1995), pp. 379–395.

Chapter 31

1. G. A. Miller, "The Magical Number Seven, Plus or Minus Two: Some Limits on Our Capacity for Processing Information," *Psychological*

Review (March 1956), pp. 81–97. See also, J. Schweickert and B. Boruff, "Short-Term Memory Capacity: Magic Number or Magic Spell?" *Journal of Experimental Psychology: Learning, Memory, and Cognition* (July 1986), pp. 419–425; and J. N. MacGregor, "Short-Term Memory Capacity: Limitation or Optimization?" *Psychological Review* (January 1987), pp. 107–108.

2. A. Bastardi and E. Shafir, "Nonconsequential Reasoning and Its Consequences," *Current Directions in Psychological Science* (December 2000), pp. 216–219.

Chapter 32

1. O. E. Tykocinski and T. S. Pittman, "The Consequences of Doing Nothing: Inaction Inertia as Avoidance of Anticipated Counterfactual Regret," *Journal of Personality and Social Psychology* (September 1998), pp. 607–616.

2. See, for instance, M. Zeelenberg, W. W. van Dijk, A. S. R. Manstead, and J. van der Pligt, "On Bad Decisions and Disconfirmed Expectancies: The Psychology of Regret and Disappointment," *Cognition and Emotion* (July 2000), pp. 521–541; and M. Zeelenberg, K. van den Bos, E. van Dijk, and R. Pieters, "The Inaction Effect in the Psychology of Regret," *Journal of Personality and Social Psychology* (March 2002), pp. 314–327.

3. M. Zeelenberg, "Anticipated Regret, Expected Feedback and Behavioral Decision Making," *Journal of Behavioral Decision Making* (June 1999), pp. 93–106.

4. M. Spranca, E. Minsk, and J. Baron, "Omission and Commission in Judgment and Choice," *Journal of Experimental Social Psychology* (January 1991), pp. 76–105.

5. V. H. Medvec, S. F. Madey, and T. Gilovich, "When Less Is More: Counterfactual Thinking and Satisfaction Among Olympic Medalists," *Journal of Personality and Social Psychology* (October 1995), pp. 603–610.

6. M. Zeelenberg, "Anticipated Regret, Expected Feedback and Behavioral Decision Making," pp. 102–103.

Chapter 33

1. R. N. Taylor and M. D. Dunnette, "Influence of Dogmatism, Risk-Taking Propensity, and Intelligence on Decision-Making Strategies for a Sample of Industrial Managers," *Journal of Applied Psychology* (August 1974), pp. 420–423.

2. V. H. Vroom and B. Pahl, "Relationship Between Age and Risk Taking Among Managers," *Journal of Applied Psychology* (October 1971), pp. 399–405.

3. D. Kahneman and A. Tversky, "Prospect Theory: An Analysis of Decision Under Risk," *Econometrica* (March 1979), pp. 263–91; and C.H. Coombs and P. E. Lehner, "Conjoint Design and Analysis of the Bilinear Model: An Application of Judgments of Risk," *Journal of Mathematical Psychology* (March 1984), pp. 1–42.

4. H. Shefrin and M. Statman, "The Disposition to Sell Winners Too Early and Ride Losers Too Long: Theory and Evidence," *Journal of Finance* (July 1985), pp. 777–791.

5. D. A. Moore, T. R. Kurtzberg, C. R. Fox, and M. H. Bazerman, "Positive Illusions and Forecasting Errors in Mutual Fund Investment Decisions," *Organizational Behavior and Human Decision Processes* (August 1999), pp. 95–114.

Chapter 34

1. "Famous Failures" cited in www.cybergrrl.com and www.entrepreneur.com.

2. B. F. Skinner, *The Behavior of Organisms: An Experimental Analysis* (New York: Appleton-Century-Crofts, 1938); eds W. K. Honig and J. E. R. Staddon, *Handbook of Operant Behavior* (Englewood Cliffs, NJ: Prentice Hall, 1977).

3. A. Ellis, "The Role of Irrational Beliefs in Perfectionism," in *Perfectionism: Theory, Research, and Treatment*, eds. G. L. Gordon and P.L. Hewitt (Washington, D.C.: American Psychological Association, 2002), pp. 217–229.

4. R. O. Frost, P. Marten, C. Lahart, and R. Rosenblate, "The Dimensions of Perfectionism," *Cognitive Therapy and Research* (October 1990), pp. 449–468.

5. K. R. Blankstein, G. L. Flett, P.L. Hewitt, and A. Eng, "Dimensions of Perfectionism and Irrational Fears: An Examination with the Fear Survey Schedule," *Personality and Individual Differences* (September 1993), pp. 323–328.

6. R. O. Frost, P. Martin, C. Lahart, and R. Rosenblate, "The Dimensions of Perfectionism."

Chapter 35

1. Based on B. Breen, "What's Your Intuition?" *Fast Company*, September 2000, pp. 290–300.

2. See, for instance, R. N. Taylor, "Age and Experience as Determinants of Managerial Information Processing and Decision Making Performance," *Academy of Management Journal* (March 1975), pp. 74–81; and M. A. Neale and G. B. Northcraft, "Experience, Expertise, and Decision Bias in Negotiation: The Role of Strategic

Conceptualization," in *Research on Negotiations in Organizations*, vol. 2, eds B. Sheppard, M. Bazerman, and R. Lewicki (Greenwich, CN: JAI Press, 1989); and M. A. Quinones, J. K. Ford, and M. S. Teachout, "The Relationship Between Work Experience and Job Performance: A Conceptual and Meta-Analytic Review," *Personnel Psychology* (Winter 1995), pp. 887–910.

3. A. Tversky and D. Kahneman, "Rational Choice and the Framing of Decisions," in *Decision Making: Descriptive, Normative, and Prescriptive Interactions*, eds D. E. Bell and H. Raiffa (New York: Cambridge University Press, 1988), pp. 167–192.

4. J. E. Russo and P. J. H. Schoemaker, *Winning Decisions* (New York: Doubleday, 2002), p. 198.

5. See, for instance, S. J. Hoch, "Combining Models with Intuition to Improve Decisions," in *Wharton on Decision Making*, eds S. J. Hoch and H.C. Kunreuther (New York: Wiley, 2001), p. 97.

6. P. Slovic, B. Fischhoff, and S. Lichtenstein, "Facts versus Fears: Understanding Perceived Risk," in *Judgment Under Uncertainty: Heuristics and Biases*, eds D. Kahneman, P. Slovic, and A. Tversky (New York: Cambridge University Press, 1982), p. 467.

7. See, for instance, W. McKelvey, *Outside the Box* (Ship Bottom, NJ: Eclipse Publishing, 1998).

Chapter 36

1. Some of these insights on Saudi culture came from P. R. Harris and R. T. Moran, *Managing Cultural Differences*, 5th ed. (Houston: Gulf Publishing, 1999), pp. 383–407.

2. See, for instance, F. Kluckhohn and F. L. Strodtbeck, *Variations in Value Orientations* (Evanston, IL: Row, Peterson, 1961); G. Hofstede, *Culture's Consequences: International Differences in Work Related*

Values (Beverly Hills, CA: Sage, 1980); and M. Javidan and R. J. House, "Cultural Acumen for the Global Manager: Lessons From Project GLOBE," *Organizational Dynamics* (Spring 2001), pp. 289–305.

3. C. K. Hsee and E. U. Weber, "Cross-National Differences in Risk Preference and Lay Predictions," *Journal of Behavioral Decision Making* (June 1999), pp. 165–179.